The Internet: Your Global Entry for Your Message and Product

Jeremy Lopez

The Internet: Your Global Entry for Your Message and Product

Published by Dr. Jeremy Lopez

ENDORSEMENTS

Jeremy does an excellent job of giving balanced instruction on how to meditate, and also explaining the benefits that come from having a regular meditation and mindfulness practice. I love how Jeremy is not afraid to learn from and quote those outside the Christian tradition. He is able to explain the ancient concepts simply from a Biblical perspective. – Kari Browning, Director, *The Beautiful Revolution*

You are put on this earth with incredible potential and a divine destiny. This powerful, practical man shows you how to tap into power you did not even know you had. – Brian Tracy – Author, *The Power of Self Confidence*

I found myself savoring the concepts of the Law of Attraction merging with the Law of Creativity until slowly the beautiful truths seeped deeper into my thirsty soul. I am called to be a Creator! My friend, Dr. Jeremy Lopez, has a way of reminding us of our eternal 'I-Am-ness' while putting the tools in our hands to unlock our endless creative potential with the Divine mind. As a musical composer, I am excited to explore, with greater understanding, the infinite realm of possibilities as I place fingers on my piano and whisper, 'Let there be!' – Dony McGuire, Grammy Award winning artist and musical composer

Jeremy dives deep into the power of consciousness and shows us that we can create a world where the champion within us can shine and how we can manifest our desires to live a life of fulfillment. A must read! – Greg S. Reid – *Forbes* and *Inc.* top rated Keynote Speaker

I have been privileged to know Jeremy Lopez for many years, as well as sharing the platform with him at a number of conferences. Through this time, I have found him as a man of integrity, commitment, wisdom, and one of the most networked people I have met. Jeremy is an entrepreneur and a leader of leaders. He has amazing insights into leadership competencies and values. He has a passion to ignite this latent potential within individuals and organizations and provide ongoing development and coaching to bring about competitive advantage and success. I would highly recommend him as a speaker, coach, mentor, and consultant. – Chris Gaborit – Learning Leader, Trainer

Dr. Jeremy Lopez's book Universal Laws: Are They Biblical? is a breath of fresh air and much needed to answer the questions that people have been asking about the correlation between Biblical and Universal Laws. I have known Jeremy Lopez for years, and as a Biblical scholar, he gives an in-depth explanation and understanding of the perfect blending and merging into the secrets and mysteries of these miraculous Laws and how Bible-based the Universal Laws truly are. As the show host for the past twelve years on The Law of Attraction Radio Network, this book answers questions that I have received from Christian and spiritual seekers around the globe about the relationship between the metaphysical and Biblical truths. After reading this book, readers will feel empowered and have strong faith that God has indeed given us these Bible-based Universal and Divine Laws to tap into so that we can live and create an abundant life. – Constance Arnold, M.A., Author, Speaker, Professional Counselor, Host of *The Think, Believe & Manifest Talk Show*

TABLE OF CONTENTS

Introduction

Welcome to *The Internet: Your Global Entry for Your Message and Product*. In an era defined by unprecedented connectivity and technological advancements, the Internet has emerged as an unparalleled platform, transforming the way we communicate, connect, and conduct business. It has revolutionized the world, breaking down geographical barriers and empowering individuals, entrepreneurs, and businesses to share their message and promote their products on a global scale.

This book is a comprehensive guide that navigates the vast digital landscape, offering insights and strategies to harness the power of the Internet effectively. Whether you are an aspiring writer, an ambitious entrepreneur, or a seasoned marketer, this book will equip you with the knowledge and tools necessary to leverage the limitless opportunities presented by the online realm.

In the following pages, we will explore the intricacies of the Internet, delving into its evolution and impact on society. We will unravel the mechanisms behind building a compelling online presence, reaching your target audience, and driving meaningful engagement. You will discover the secrets to crafting a persuasive message that resonates with your audience, as well as tactics to establish a credible brand identity amidst the digital noise.

The Internet: Your Global Entry for Your Message and Product is more than just a manual for online success. It is a roadmap that encourages you to embrace the ever-changing nature of the Internet and adapt your strategies accordingly. From social media marketing and content creation to search engine optimization and e-commerce, this book will provide you with actionable insights to stay ahead in a dynamic digital landscape.

Prepare to embark on a journey that will empower you to unlock the full potential of the Internet, transforming your message into a global force and your product into a sought-after commodity. Embrace the opportunities that lie within your reach, seize the power of connectivity, and embark on an extraordinary adventure that will shape the trajectory of your personal or professional endeavors.

Are you ready to unleash the power of the Internet and propel your message and product to unprecedented heights? Let's embark on this transformative journey together.

The internet is a wondrous creation, a global network of interconnected computers that allows you to access a wealth of knowledge and connect with people across continents. It transcends physical boundaries, enabling you to explore new cultures, ideas, and perspectives with just a few clicks.

In the past, the world seemed vast and unreachable, but the internet has changed everything. It has revolutionized the way we communicate, bridging gaps and making the world a smaller place. Through social media platforms, video calls, and instant messaging services, you can connect with friends, family, and even strangers from any part of the world. It has never been easier to build relationships and learn from diverse cultures.

The internet is a treasure trove of knowledge that transcends the limitations of traditional libraries and educational institutions. With search engines and online databases at your fingertips, you can explore any topic imaginable. Want to learn about ancient civilizations, delve into scientific breakthroughs, or understand the intricacies of art? The internet has it all. Online courses and tutorials provide opportunities for personal and professional growth, empowering you to develop new skills and broaden your horizons.

The internet has transformed the way we conduct business. With e-commerce platforms, you can purchase products from around the world, explore unique handicrafts, or discover exotic cuisines without leaving your home. Small businesses and entrepreneurs now have access to a global marketplace, enabling them to reach customers far beyond their local communities.

In the past, news traveled slowly, but the internet has made information instantaneous. Breaking news from across the globe reaches you within seconds, allowing you to stay informed about global events. With access to a plethora of online news sources, you can explore different perspectives and gain a broader understanding of world affairs.

The internet has become a platform for cultural exchange and self-expression. Social media, blogs, and video-sharing platforms empower individuals to share their thoughts, ideas, and creations with a worldwide audience. Through this digital medium, artists, writers, musicians, and influencers can connect with fans and followers from every corner of the world, fostering a global appreciation for diverse forms of art and culture.

Traveling the world has never been easier thanks to the internet. Through virtual tours, interactive maps, and immersive videos, you can explore famous landmarks, visit museums, and experience different destinations from the comfort of your own home. While nothing can replace the magic of physical travel, the internet offers a glimpse into new places and ignites the desire to embark on real-world adventures.

The internet has revolutionized collaboration, enabling individuals and organizations to work together regardless of geographical barriers. Remote work, online collaboration tools, and video conferencing platforms have transformed the way we do business. Experts from diverse fields can now come together, share knowledge, and solve global challenges collaboratively.

As we navigate the vastness of the internet, it is crucial to be responsible digital citizens. Respecting privacy, sharing reliable information, and fostering a positive online environment are essential to ensure the internet remains a safe and inclusive space for everyone.

The internet is an extraordinary gateway to the world, offering unparalleled opportunities for connectivity, knowledge sharing, and cultural exchange. It has revolutionized the way we communicate, learn, and conduct business, breaking down geographical barriers and bringing people together like never before. However, it's important to approach this gateway with caution, responsibility, and an understanding of the potential risks that come with it.

As you embark on your journey through the internet, keep the following principles in mind:

The internet connects us with individuals from all walks of life, cultures, and backgrounds. Embrace this diversity and treat others with respect, kindness, and empathy. Engage in constructive discussions and learn from different perspectives, fostering an inclusive and positive online environment.

With an abundance of information available online, it's crucial to develop critical thinking skills and verify the accuracy of the information you encounter. Be mindful of misinformation, fact-check sources, and rely on reputable platforms for news, research, and knowledge acquisition.

As you explore the internet, be aware of your digital footprint. Safeguard your personal information, use strong passwords, and be cautious about sharing sensitive data. Understand privacy settings on social media platforms and be mindful of the information you choose to share.

Respect copyright laws, intellectual property rights, and the creative work of others. Give proper credit when using or sharing content that belongs to someone else. Avoid engaging in cyberbullying, harassment, or any form of harmful behavior that can negatively impact individuals or communities.

While the internet offers incredible opportunities, it's essential to find a balance between your online and offline experiences. Engage in real-world interactions, pursue hobbies, and nurture meaningful relationships beyond the digital realm. Remember that the richness of life lies in experiencing the world firsthand.

By embracing these principles, you can fully harness the power of the internet as your gateway to the world while contributing to a positive and responsible digital community.

The internet has leveled the playing field, offering unparalleled opportunities for individuals to become digital entrepreneurs. Whether you have a unique product, a creative service, or a message to share, the internet provides a platform to showcase your offerings to a global audience. It allows you to break free from traditional geographical limitations and connect with customers and clients worldwide.

Establishing a strong online presence is vital in leveraging the internet as a gateway to share your message and products. Start by creating a professional website or online store that showcases your offerings in an engaging and user-friendly manner. Utilize social media platforms to connect with your target audience, share valuable content, and build a community around your brand.

The internet provides unprecedented opportunities to connect directly with your target audience. Through social media, email marketing, and content creation, you can engage with your followers, understand their needs and preferences, and tailor your message and products to meet their expectations. This direct line of communication allows for authentic and meaningful interactions, fostering trust and loyalty.

In a crowded digital landscape, storytelling becomes a powerful tool to captivate your audience and differentiate your brand. Share your journey, your values, and the inspiration behind your message or products. Through compelling storytelling, you can create an emotional connection with your audience, driving engagement and fostering brand loyalty.

Digital marketing strategies open up endless possibilities for promoting your message and products. Harness the power of search engine optimization (SEO) to increase your online visibility and reach. Utilize pay-per-click advertising, influencer collaborations, and email campaigns to expand your reach and attract new customers. Data analytics tools provide valuable insights into customer behavior, allowing you to refine your marketing strategies and maximize your impact.

E-commerce has revolutionized the way products are bought and sold. With the internet as your gateway, you can establish an online store, reach customers worldwide, and streamline the sales process. From physical products to digital downloads, the internet enables you to showcase and sell your offerings with ease. Leverage secure payment gateways and robust logistics solutions to provide a seamless customer experience.

Content creation is a cornerstone of online success. Whether through blogging, podcasting, video production, or social media content, you can share your expertise, educate your audience, and build trust in your brand. Valuable and engaging content not only attracts new customers but also establishes you as an authority in your field.

The internet breaks down geographical barriers, enabling you to tap into a global marketplace. Local businesses can expand their reach internationally, while individuals can share their creative works with a global audience. Embrace the opportunity to connect with people from different cultures and backgrounds, fostering a sense of unity and collaboration.

The internet is a dynamic and ever-evolving space. To thrive in this digital landscape, it's essential to stay adaptable and embrace innovation. Continuously monitor industry trends, embrace emerging technologies, and be open to experimenting with new strategies. By staying ahead of the curve, you can remain competitive and maximize the impact of your message and products.

The internet serves as a gateway to amplify your message and products, providing you with unparalleled opportunities to reach a global audience, establish your brand, and make a lasting impact. By building a strong online presence, connecting with your target audience, and leveraging digital marketing strategies, you can effectively share your message and showcase your products to the world.

Remember, authenticity and storytelling are key. Share your unique story, values, and passion behind your message or products. Engage with your audience, listen to their feedback, and create a community around your brand. By nurturing this connection, you can foster loyalty and turn customers into advocates.

In the world of e-commerce, capitalize on the convenience and accessibility it offers. Create an online store that is user-friendly, visually appealing, and showcases your products in the best light. Leverage secure payment gateways and efficient logistics to provide a seamless customer experience, regardless of their location.

Content creation is a powerful tool to engage your audience and establish your expertise. Create valuable and engaging content through various mediums such as blog posts, podcasts, videos, or social media. Share insights, tips, and stories that resonate with your audience and establish you as a trusted authority in your field.

Embrace the global marketplace and seize opportunities to connect with individuals from diverse cultures and backgrounds. Adapt your message and products to resonate with different markets while staying true to your brand identity. Embracing diversity and fostering inclusive practices will not only expand your reach but also enrich your brand's value.

Stay adaptable and innovative in this ever-evolving digital landscape. Continuously monitor industry trends, experiment with new strategies, and leverage emerging technologies to stay ahead of the competition. Data analytics and customer feedback will provide valuable insights to refine your approach and maximize your impact.

The internet is an incredible gateway that can catapult your message and products onto the global stage. It empowers you to share your unique voice, reach a vast audience, and leave a lasting impression. Embrace the power of the internet, harness its limitless possibilities, and let your message and products shine in the digital realm. Your journey to make an impact on the world starts now.

A Global Gateway to Success

In the digital age, the internet has revolutionized the way we live, work, and connect with one another. One of its most significant impacts has been on the world of business. With the advent of the internet, doors that were once closed have swung wide open, creating endless opportunities for businesses to thrive in ways never before imaginable. This chapter explores how the internet has transformed the business landscape, enabling organizations to reach new markets, streamline operations, enhance customer experiences, and foster innovation.

The internet has dissolved geographical boundaries and presented businesses with a vast global marketplace. Previously, small businesses were limited to their local communities, but now, they can reach customers around the world with a simple click of a button. E-commerce platforms have empowered entrepreneurs to establish online storefronts, enabling them to sell products and services to a global customer base. The ability to tap into new markets has resulted in unprecedented growth and revenue streams for businesses of all sizes.

The internet has brought about significant efficiencies in business operations. Communication and collaboration have become seamless, allowing teams to work together regardless of their physical locations. Email, instant messaging, video conferencing, and project management tools have revolutionized the way organizations operate, enabling faster decision-making and increased productivity. Furthermore, cloud computing has provided businesses with scalable and cost-effective solutions for storage, data management, and software applications. These technological advancements have reduced operational costs and streamlined processes, allowing businesses to focus on their core competencies.

With the internet, businesses can now engage with their customers on a whole new level. Online platforms, social media, and review websites have given customers a voice, allowing them to share their experiences and opinions with the world. This instant feedback loop enables businesses to understand their customers better, tailor their products and services to meet their needs, and build strong brand loyalty. Additionally, businesses can provide personalized experiences through targeted marketing, recommendation systems, and customer relationship management tools. The internet has transformed the way businesses interact with customers, placing their satisfaction and engagement at the forefront.

The internet has become a breeding ground for innovation. It has democratized access to information, allowing entrepreneurs and inventors to learn from global best practices and collaborate with experts from diverse fields. Crowdsourcing platforms have facilitated the collective wisdom of the masses, enabling businesses to gather ideas, funding, and feedback from a wide range of individuals. Open-source software and collaborative development tools have sparked creativity and accelerated the pace of innovation. The internet has not only opened doors for existing businesses to thrive but has also paved the way for countless startups and disruptive ventures to enter the market.

While the internet has undeniably opened doorways for business to thrive, it is essential to acknowledge the challenges and considerations that come with it. Online security threats, data privacy concerns, and information overload are issues that businesses must address to ensure a safe and trustworthy digital environment. Moreover, as the internet continues to evolve, businesses must adapt to changing technologies, consumer behaviors, and market trends to remain competitive.

The internet has transformed the business landscape, creating unprecedented opportunities for organizations to thrive. It has expanded market reach, streamlined operations, enhanced customer experiences, and fostered innovation. Businesses of all sizes can now leverage the power of the internet to access global markets, collaborate seamlessly, and connect with customers like never before. As we move further into the digital era, businesses must embrace the internet's potential while navigating its challenges to stay at the forefront of this ever-evolving landscape.

Personally, I think back to the time when the internet was still in its infancy. Although I had a vision to reach the world through the outreach of Identity Network, it wasn't until the internet became part of daily life that such an undertaking became a very real reality. Right now, you have the entire globe literally at your fingertips.

In this chapter, we will explore how the internet has become a powerful gateway to success in the world of business. In today's digital age, leveraging the vast opportunities offered by the online realm is crucial for achieving and sustaining business success. Whether you're an aspiring entrepreneur, a small business owner, or a corporate professional, understanding the potential of the internet is essential for growth and prosperity. Let's dive in!

The internet has revolutionized the way businesses operate by providing a global reach like never before. With a few clicks, your products and services can reach millions of potential customers around the world. This accessibility transcends geographical boundaries and time zones, opening up opportunities for business expansion and international growth. Whether you're a small local business or a multinational corporation, the internet offers an unparalleled platform to showcase your offerings to a diverse audience.

Traditional marketing and advertising methods can be expensive and have limited reach. However, the internet provides cost-effective and targeted marketing solutions. Through search engine optimization (SEO), social media marketing, content marketing, and paid online advertising, businesses can precisely target their desired customer base. This level of precision allows for greater return on investment (ROI) and enables businesses to optimize their marketing efforts efficiently.

The rise of e-commerce has been one of the most significant advancements facilitated by the internet. Setting up an online store has become increasingly accessible and affordable, enabling businesses of all sizes to sell products and services online. The internet offers a convenient shopping experience for customers and provides businesses with a platform to showcase their offerings 24/7. Additionally, online marketplaces provide access to a vast customer base, boosting sales potential and revenue generation.

In today's digital landscape, having a strong online presence is crucial for business success. Establishing a professional website and engaging in active social media participation allows businesses to connect and interact with their customers directly. Through regular content creation, such as blog posts, videos, and podcasts, businesses can position themselves as industry leaders, build brand loyalty, and establish credibility. An engaged online community can become powerful brand advocates, further expanding your reach and influence.

The internet generates an enormous amount of data, providing valuable insights that can drive business growth. Through web analytics and tracking tools, businesses can gather information about customer behavior, preferences, and demographics. This data can be utilized to refine marketing strategies, optimize product offerings, and identify emerging trends. By leveraging these insights, businesses can make data-driven decisions that lead to improved customer experiences, enhanced operational efficiency, and increased profitability.

The internet has revolutionized collaboration and networking within the business world. Platforms such as LinkedIn, professional forums, and industry-specific communities allow entrepreneurs, professionals, and businesses to connect, share knowledge, and collaborate on projects. The power of networking online extends beyond borders and traditional limitations, enabling businesses to tap into a global network of talent, expertise, and potential partnerships.

The internet has transformed the business landscape, offering unprecedented opportunities for success. It has enabled businesses to reach a global audience, revolutionized marketing and sales strategies, facilitated the growth of e-commerce, empowered data-driven decision making, and revolutionized collaboration and networking. Embracing the power of the internet and leveraging its capabilities can catapult your business to new heights. So, harness the potential of this digital gateway and embrace the limitless opportunities it presents for your business success.

The internet provides businesses with a direct channel for engaging with their customers and gathering valuable feedback. Through social media platforms, online reviews, and customer support forums, businesses can interact with their audience, address concerns, and provide timely assistance. This direct line of communication not only strengthens customer relationships but also allows businesses to gain insights into customer satisfaction, preferences, and pain points. By actively listening to customer feedback, businesses can improve their products, services, and overall customer experience, leading to increased loyalty and positive word-of-mouth.

Compared to traditional brick-and-mortar operations, the internet offers significant cost savings and scalability. Online businesses can eliminate or reduce expenses related to physical storefronts, inventory management, and overhead costs. This cost efficiency allows businesses to allocate resources towards innovation, marketing, and customer acquisition. Furthermore, the internet provides the flexibility to scale operations rapidly without significant upfront investments. Businesses can adapt quickly to changing market demands and seize growth opportunities with relative ease, enabling them to stay agile and competitive.

The internet provides a vast array of business tools, resources, and platforms that can streamline operations and drive productivity. Project management software, customer relationship management (CRM) systems, cloud storage solutions, and communication platforms enable efficient collaboration, organization, and data management. Additionally, online learning platforms and industry-specific websites offer valuable educational resources, training courses, and insights into best practices. Embracing these digital resources empowers businesses to optimize processes, improve efficiency, and stay ahead in a rapidly evolving business landscape.

The internet has fueled a wave of innovation and disruption across industries. Startups and entrepreneurs can leverage the internet to challenge traditional business models, introduce groundbreaking products or services, and disrupt established markets. The accessibility of information, crowdfunding platforms, and online marketplaces have lowered barriers to entry, enabling aspiring entrepreneurs to turn their ideas into reality. The internet has democratized entrepreneurship, allowing individuals from diverse backgrounds to pursue their passions, disrupt industries, and achieve remarkable success.

The internet landscape is in a constant state of evolution, with new technologies and trends emerging at a rapid pace. Businesses that embrace innovation, adapt to changing consumer behaviors, and stay abreast of the latest digital advancements are better positioned for long-term success. It is crucial for businesses to remain agile, continuously monitor industry trends, and be open to embracing new technologies and strategies that can enhance their competitive advantage.

The internet serves as an invaluable gateway to success in the world of business. Its global reach, marketing potential, e-commerce capabilities, data-driven insights, networking opportunities, customer engagement channels, cost efficiency, scalability, access to resources, and fostering innovation are key drivers for business growth and prosperity. By harnessing the power of the internet, businesses can tap into a vast network of opportunities, connect with customers worldwide, and navigate the digital landscape with confidence. Embrace the internet as your gateway to success and unlock the immense potential it offers for your business in today's interconnected world.

From its humble origins as a research project to the global network that connects billions of people today, understanding the journey of the internet is essential to appreciate its transformative power. So, let's take a trip back in time and explore the birth and evolution of the internet.

The story of the internet begins in the mid-20th century, during the early days of computers and telecommunications. In the 1960s, researchers and scientists recognized the need for a decentralized communication network that could connect computers and exchange information. The Advanced Research Projects Agency

(ARPA), a division of the United States Department of Defense, played a pivotal role in funding and coordinating research efforts that laid the foundation for the internet.

In 1969, ARPANET was created, marking a significant milestone in the development of the internet. ARPANET, an experimental network, connected computers at various research institutions and allowed them to share data. This network was designed to be resilient, allowing information to flow even if parts of the network were damaged or destroyed—a critical characteristic that would later define the robustness of the internet.

One of the most crucial breakthroughs in the history of the internet was the development of the Transmission Control Protocol/Internet Protocol (TCP/IP) suite. In the 1970s, researchers Vinton Cerf and Robert Kahn designed TCP/IP, a set of protocols that standardized data transmission and allowed different networks to communicate with each other. TCP/IP became the foundation for the internet, providing a common language that enabled computers to exchange information across different networks.

As the internet continued to evolve, new applications and services emerged. In 1971, Ray Tomlinson introduced email, a revolutionary method of sending electronic messages across the network. Email quickly became one of the most widely used and essential communication tools on the internet. Additionally, the Domain Name System (DNS) was created to translate human-readable domain names into IP addresses, making it easier for people to access websites and services on the internet.

In the 1980s, ARPANET was decommissioned, and its successor, the Internet Protocol network, came into existence. The internet started expanding beyond academic and research institutions, gradually becoming accessible to a broader audience. The development of commercial internet service providers (ISPs) in the late 1980s and early 1990s made it possible for individuals and businesses to connect to the internet from their homes and offices, further fueling its growth.

While the internet was evolving, another significant development took place—the creation of the World Wide Web. In 1989, Tim Berners-Lee, a British computer scientist, invented the World Wide Web, a system of interlinked hypertext documents accessible via the internet. The web introduced a user-friendly interface, hyperlinks, and the concept of web pages, revolutionizing how people accessed and shared information online. The web's intuitive design and ease of use played a vital role in popularizing the internet and driving its widespread adoption.

As the 21st century dawned, the internet rapidly expanded its reach across the globe. With advancements in telecommunications infrastructure, increased bandwidth, and the proliferation of mobile devices, the internet became an integral part of everyday life for billions of people worldwide. It transformed various aspects of society, including communication, commerce, education, entertainment, and governance, connecting individuals, businesses and governments on an unprecedented scale.

The widespread adoption of smartphones and the advent of mobile internet further accelerated the internet's growth. Mobile devices equipped with internet connectivity became ubiquitous, allowing people to access the internet anytime, anywhere. This mobile revolution enabled new opportunities for communication, social networking, mobile applications, and mobile commerce, transforming the way we interact with the digital world.

Simultaneously, the evolution of broadband technology revolutionized internet speeds and capabilities. High-speed broadband connections became more affordable and accessible, enabling seamless streaming of media, video conferencing, cloud computing, and the emergence of bandwidth-intensive applications. The increased bandwidth paved the way for richer online experiences and facilitated the development of innovative services and platforms.

The rise of social media platforms introduced a new era of user-generated content and online social interaction. Websites such as Facebook, Twitter, Instagram, and YouTube enabled individuals to connect, share, and collaborate with others on a global scale. Social media transformed the way we communicate, disseminate information, and engage with brands, creating new opportunities for businesses to reach and engage with their target audience.

Another significant development in recent years has been the emergence of the Internet of Things (IoT). The IoT refers to the interconnection of everyday physical devices, vehicles, appliances, and other objects embedded with sensors, software, and network connectivity. These connected devices can communicate, collect and exchange data, and perform tasks autonomously, revolutionizing industries such as healthcare, transportation, manufacturing, and smart homes. The IoT has expanded the internet's reach beyond computers and mobile devices, creating a vast network of interconnected objects that further integrates the digital and physical worlds.

As the internet evolved, so did the challenges related to security and privacy. With the increased connectivity and the exchange of sensitive information online, the need for robust cybersecurity measures became paramount. Cyber threats, such as hacking, data breaches, and identity theft, prompted the development of sophisticated security protocols, encryption techniques, and privacy regulations to safeguard users' data and protect online transactions. Ensuring a secure and trusted internet environment remains an ongoing priority for individuals, businesses, and governments.

The internet's birth and evolution have transformed the world, revolutionizing communication, information exchange, and the way we conduct business. From its early origins as a research project to its global reach connecting billions of people, the internet has become an indispensable part of our daily lives. Its continued growth, technological advancements, and the ever-expanding range of possibilities it offers present a world of opportunities and challenges. Understanding the journey of the internet helps us appreciate its immense impact and adapt to its constantly evolving landscape, shaping the future of our digital interconnected world. Now, the entire globe is at your fingertips. Use your power wisely.

Navigating the Digital Landscape

In today's fast-paced and interconnected world, the digital landscape has become a vital aspect of conducting business. The Internet and various digital technologies have transformed the way organizations operate, communicate, and engage with customers. To thrive in this digital era, it is crucial for businesses to navigate the digital landscape effectively. In this chapter, we will explore key strategies and considerations to help you successfully navigate the digital landscape in your business endeavors.

Digital transformation is not merely a buzzword; it is a fundamental shift that affects all aspects of business. To navigate the digital landscape, you must embrace this transformation by integrating digital technologies into your operations, products, and services. This could involve implementing cloud computing, adopting data analytics, leveraging artificial intelligence, or utilizing social media and mobile platforms. Embracing digital transformation ensures that your business stays relevant, competitive, and able to meet the evolving demands of the digital age.

In the digital landscape, understanding your target audience is crucial. Take the time to identify who your customers are, their preferences, behaviors, and pain points. Use analytics tools, conduct surveys, or engage with customers directly to gain insights. This understanding will enable you to tailor your digital marketing efforts, create personalized experiences, and deliver value to your customers. Remember, the digital landscape offers a wealth of data and tools to help you gain a deep understanding of your target audience.

Having a strong online presence is paramount for navigating the digital landscape. Start by creating a professional and user-friendly website that reflects your brand identity. Optimize it for search engines to increase visibility. Leverage social media platforms, such as Facebook, Twitter, LinkedIn, and Instagram, to engage with your target audience, share valuable content, and build a community. Additionally, consider utilizing other online channels, such as email marketing, search engine marketing (SEM), and content marketing, to expand your reach and attract new customers.

User experience (UX) plays a vital role in the success of your digital initiatives. Ensure that your website and digital interfaces are intuitive, responsive, and easy to navigate. Pay attention to loading times, mobile optimization, and accessibility for all users. Implement a seamless checkout process for e-commerce platforms, and provide multiple support channels to address customer queries promptly. By prioritizing UX, you will enhance customer satisfaction, loyalty, and ultimately drive business growth.

Data is a goldmine in the digital landscape. Collecting and analyzing data can provide valuable insights into customer behavior, market trends, and operational efficiency. Utilize data analytics tools to track website traffic, monitor social media engagement, and measure key performance indicators (KPIs). Analyze the data to make informed decisions, identify areas for improvement, and optimize your digital strategies. Data-driven decision-making will help you stay ahead of the competition and drive meaningful results.

The digital landscape is ever-evolving, with new technologies and trends emerging regularly. To navigate successfully, you must stay agile and adaptable. Keep a pulse on industry developments, follow thought leaders, attend relevant conferences, and participate in online communities. Foster a culture of innovation within your organization, encouraging employees to explore new ideas and experiment with digital tools. By staying agile and adaptable, you can proactively respond to changes, seize opportunities, and maintain a competitive edge.

Navigating the digital landscape in business requires a proactive approach, an understanding of your target audience, and a willingness to adapt. By embracing digital transformation, building a strong online presence, prioritizing user experience, leveraging data analytics, and staying agile, you can effectively navigate the digital landscape and drive your business forward in the digital era. It's important to remember that the digital landscape is not a one-time endeavor but an ongoing process. As technology advances and customer expectations evolve, you must continuously reassess your digital strategies and make adjustments accordingly.

With the increased reliance on digital technologies comes the need for robust cybersecurity measures. Protecting sensitive data, customer information, and intellectual property is paramount. Implement strong security protocols, employ encryption methods, and regularly update your systems to safeguard against cyber threats. Educate your employees about best practices for online security and establish clear guidelines to prevent data breaches. By prioritizing cybersecurity, you can mitigate risks and build trust with your customers.

The digital landscape offers numerous opportunities for collaboration and partnerships.

Look for ways to collaborate with complementary businesses, influencers, or industry experts to expand your reach and tap into new markets. Seek partnerships with technology providers or digital agencies that can help enhance your digital capabilities. By forging strategic alliances, you can leverage expertise, share resources, and achieve mutual growth in the digital landscape.

In the digital realm, feedback and reviews have a significant impact on your reputation. Actively monitor online platforms, review sites, and social media channels to gauge customer sentiment and respond to feedback promptly. Addressing customer concerns, resolving issues, and acknowledging positive feedback demonstrates your commitment to customer satisfaction. Engaging with your audience in a transparent and authentic manner builds trust and fosters long-term relationships.

The digital landscape is constantly evolving, making it essential to prioritize continuous learning and innovation. Encourage your team to stay updated on industry trends, emerging technologies, and digital marketing strategies. Invest in employee training and development programs to enhance digital skills within your organization. Foster a culture that embraces experimentation and rewards innovative thinking. By continuously learning and innovating, you can stay ahead of the curve and seize new opportunities in the dynamic digital landscape.

Navigating the digital landscape in business requires a comprehensive approach that encompasses embracing digital transformation, understanding your target audience, developing a strong online presence, prioritizing user experience, leveraging data analytics, staying agile and adaptable, investing in cybersecurity, fostering collaboration and partnerships, monitoring online feedback, and continuously learning and innovating. By incorporating these strategies into your business practices, you can effectively navigate the digital landscape and position your organization for success in the digital era.

With the increasing use of smartphones and tablets, mobile optimization is crucial for businesses in the digital landscape. Ensure that your website, emails, and digital content are responsive and optimized for mobile devices. Mobile-friendly interfaces and seamless user experiences are vital to engage with the growing number of mobile users. Invest in mobile apps or progressive web applications (PWAs) to provide a convenient and personalized experience for your customers on the go.

Automation and artificial intelligence (AI) technologies can greatly streamline and enhance your digital operations. Implement chatbots or virtual assistants to provide instant customer support and handle routine inquiries. Utilize AI algorithms to analyze customer data, personalize recommendations, and automate marketing campaigns. Automation not only saves time and resources but also enables you to deliver faster, more efficient services to your customers.

In the digital landscape, influencer marketing has become a powerful tool for reaching and engaging with your target audience. Identify influential individuals in your industry or niche who have a strong online presence and a relevant following. Collaborate with them to promote your products or services through sponsored content or partnerships. Influencers can help amplify your brand message, increase brand awareness, and drive conversions.

In the digital age, maintaining a positive online reputation is vital. Monitor mentions of your brand across various online platforms and respond promptly to any negative feedback or reviews. Implement online reputation management strategies to proactively address issues, protect your brand image, and maintain credibility. Engage in proactive brand building activities, such as thought leadership articles, guest blogging, and participating in industry forums, to shape a positive perception of your business in the digital landscape.

The digital landscape is constantly evolving with the emergence of new technologies. Stay informed about emerging trends, such as blockchain, virtual reality (VR), augmented reality (AR), or the Internet of Things (IoT). Assess how these technologies can be integrated into your business to improve efficiency, enhance customer experiences, or open up new revenue streams. Being proactive in exploring and adopting emerging technologies can give your business a competitive edge and position you as an industry leader.

Collaborating with digital partners can significantly enhance your business capabilities. These partners may include technology providers, digital marketing agencies, e-commerce platforms, or data analytics firms. Build strong relationships with reliable partners who can support your digital initiatives, offer expertise, and help you stay at the forefront of digital innovation. A strong network of digital partners can provide valuable resources, insights, and collaborative opportunities to navigate the digital landscape successfully.

As data privacy regulations become more stringent, it is crucial to stay compliant in your digital operations. Familiarize yourself with regulations such as the General Data Protection Regulation (GDPR) and the California Consumer Privacy Act (CCPA), and ensure that your data collection, storage, and processing practices align with these requirements. Prioritize transparency and consent when collecting customer data, and implement robust data security measures to protect sensitive information. Compliance with data privacy regulations not only protects your customers but also helps build trust and credibility for your business.

Navigating the digital landscape in business requires a comprehensive and dynamic approach that encompasses mobile optimization, automation, influencer marketing, online reputation management, emerging technologies, digital partnerships, data privacy compliance, and more. By embracing these strategies, continually adapting to technological advancements, and keeping your finger on the pulse of the digital landscape, you can position your business for success in the digital era.

Remember, the digital landscape is ever-evolving, so it's crucial to remain agile, innovative, and customer-centric to thrive in this dynamic environment.

In the digital landscape, customers interact with businesses through multiple channels, including websites, social media, email, mobile apps, and physical stores. Embracing omnichannel marketing ensures a seamless and consistent customer experience across all touchpoints. Integrate your marketing efforts across channels, align messaging, and leverage customer data to provide personalized experiences. By adopting an omnichannel approach, you can engage customers at various touchpoints and increase brand loyalty.

Content marketing plays a crucial role in attracting and engaging customers in the digital landscape. Develop a content strategy that focuses on creating valuable, relevant, and engaging content to educate, entertain, or solve customer problems. Publish blog posts, articles, videos, podcasts, and infographics to showcase your expertise and build trust with your audience. Optimize content for search engines to improve visibility and drive organic traffic to your website. A strong content marketing strategy can position your business as a thought leader and drive customer engagement.

In the digital landscape, building strong relationships with your customers is essential. Actively engage with your audience through social media, online communities, and interactive content. Respond to comments, queries, and reviews promptly to demonstrate your commitment to customer satisfaction. Encourage customer feedback and testimonials to foster a sense of community and build brand advocacy. Engaged and satisfied customers can become brand ambassadors, driving word-of-mouth marketing and attracting new customers to your business.

Monitoring and analyzing key metrics is crucial for navigating the digital landscape effectively. Utilize web analytics tools to track website traffic, user behavior, conversion rates, and campaign performance. Leverage social media analytics to measure engagement, reach, and the effectiveness of your social media efforts. Regularly review these metrics to gain insights into the success of your digital initiatives, identify areas for improvement, and make data-driven decisions to optimize your strategies.

Data is a valuable asset in the digital landscape, and cultivating a data-driven culture within your organization is essential. Encourage employees to collect and analyze data, use data insights to drive decision-making, and measure the impact of digital strategies. Invest in training programs to enhance data literacy among your team members. By leveraging data effectively, you can uncover valuable insights, identify trends, and make informed decisions that drive business growth.

In the digital landscape, ethical behavior and transparency are critical for maintaining trust with customers and stakeholders. Clearly communicate your privacy policies, data handling practices, and terms of service. Obtain proper consent when collecting customer data and adhere to data protection regulations. Be transparent about sponsored content, advertising, or partnerships to maintain authenticity and credibility. By operating ethically and transparently, you can build long-term relationships with customers and foster a positive brand image.

Consumer behaviors and expectations evolve rapidly in the digital landscape. Stay attuned to these changes and adapt your strategies accordingly. Monitor market trends, conduct customer surveys, and engage in social listening to understand shifting preferences and needs. Embrace emerging communication platforms, new technologies, or innovative business models to meet changing consumer demands. By staying agile and responsive to consumer behaviors, you can stay ahead of the competition and seize new opportunities.

Successfully navigating the digital landscape in business requires embracing omnichannel marketing, harnessing content marketing, fostering customer engagement, monitoring key metrics, cultivating a data-driven culture, staying ethical and transparent, adapting to changing consumer behaviors, and more. By incorporating these strategies into your digital initiatives, you can effectively engage customers, drive business growth, and maintain a competitive edge in the dynamic digital landscape. Remember, the digital landscape is ever-evolving, so

In the fast-paced digital landscape, agility is crucial to keep up with rapid changes and deliver projects effectively. Adopt agile project management methodologies such as Scrum or Kanban to improve collaboration, flexibility, and efficiency within your teams. Break down projects into smaller, manageable tasks with defined timelines. Regularly review and adapt project plans based on feedback and evolving priorities. Embracing agile project management allows you to respond swiftly to market demands and deliver high-quality digital solutions.

Personalization is a powerful tool in the digital landscape to enhance customer experiences and drive engagement. Utilize customer data to create personalized recommendations, targeted marketing campaigns, and tailored content. Leverage artificial intelligence and machine learning algorithms to understand customer preferences and deliver customized experiences. By offering personalized interactions and content, you can strengthen customer relationships and drive conversions.

In the digital age, consumers are increasingly conscious of a company's social and environmental impact. Emphasize social responsibility in your digital initiatives by supporting causes, promoting sustainability, and engaging in corporate social responsibility (CSR) activities. Communicate your efforts transparently through your digital channels to build trust and resonate with socially conscious customers. Incorporating social responsibility into your digital strategy not only benefits society but also enhances your brand reputation and loyalty.

The digital landscape provides opportunities to connect with your target audience through virtual events and webinars. Host webinars on relevant topics to showcase your expertise and engage with your audience in real-time. Participate in virtual conferences, trade shows, or networking events to expand your reach and establish industry connections. Virtual events offer cost-effective and scalable ways to connect with customers, generate leads, and promote your brand.

As businesses increasingly rely on digital technologies, cybersecurity threats continue to evolve. Stay vigilant and proactive in protecting your digital assets and customer data. Implement robust cybersecurity measures such as firewalls, encryption, multi-factor authentication, and regular vulnerability assessments. Educate your employees about cybersecurity best practices, including password hygiene and phishing awareness. By prioritizing cybersecurity, you can safeguard your business and maintain the trust of your customers.

To navigate the digital landscape successfully, foster a culture of innovation within your organization. Encourage employees to think creatively, experiment with new ideas, and embrace emerging technologies. Create channels for employees to share innovative concepts and provide them with resources and support to explore and implement digital innovations. By fostering a culture of innovation, you can drive continuous improvement, adapt to changes in the digital landscape, and position your business as a forward-thinking industry leader.

Navigating the digital landscape in business requires embracing agile project management, implementing personalization and customization, emphasizing social responsibility, leveraging virtual events, prioritizing cybersecurity, fostering a culture of innovation, and more. By incorporating these strategies into your digital initiatives, you can effectively adapt to changing trends, meet customer expectations, and drive sustainable business growth in the dynamic digital landscape. Remember, staying proactive, adaptable, and customer-centric is key to thriving in the digital era.

Building Your Digital Brand

In a world overflowing with products and services, standing out from the crowd has become a challenge for businesses of all sizes. In this chapter, we will explore the captivating concept of branding and how it holds the key to creating a lasting impression on consumers. We will delve into the core principles of effective branding and showcase notable examples of brands that have successfully etched themselves into the collective consciousness.

At its essence, branding is the art of shaping perceptions. It encompasses every touchpoint and interaction a consumer has with a company, creating a cohesive and memorable experience. A strong brand cultivates loyalty, fosters trust, and evokes emotions, making it a powerful tool in capturing market share.

Memorable brands are built on a strong foundation of purpose and values. They connect with their audience by aligning their mission with the aspirations and beliefs of their target market. Patagonia, the outdoor clothing company, exemplifies this by championing environmental sustainability and responsible consumption, resonating with environmentally conscious consumers.

Visual elements play a significant role in brand recognition. Memorable brands craft a distinct identity through logos, color schemes, typography, and overall design. The iconic "swoosh" of Nike immediately evokes a sense of athleticism and empowerment, while Coca-Cola's classic red and white logo represents joy and nostalgia.

Consistency is crucial for brand recognition. Successful brands develop a clear and concise message that remains consistent across all channels and touchpoints. Apple's "Think Different" campaign, coupled with its minimalist product design, has established a consistent and distinctive brand voice.

The most impactful brands evoke emotions, forging a deep connection with consumers. Airbnb has succeeded in creating an emotional bond by emphasizing the sense of belonging and the spirit of adventure that their platform enables. Through heartfelt storytelling, they have become more than just a booking platform—they embody the desire for meaningful experiences.

Known for its sleek and innovative products, Apple has cultivated a fiercely loyal customer base. The brand's focus on simplicity, elegance, and user experience has made Apple synonymous with cutting-edge technology and premium quality.

Google has become synonymous with internet search and has expanded its brand into various digital services. Through its minimalist and user-friendly interface, Google has positioned itself as the go-to source for information and has even become a verb in everyday language.

Since its inception, Coca-Cola has successfully established itself as the ultimate refreshing beverage. Its timeless brand image, coupled with engaging marketing campaigns and emotional storytelling, has made Coca-Cola a symbol of happiness and togetherness.

Nike's iconic "Just Do It" slogan has inspired millions worldwide. The brand's association with high-performance athletes and its commitment to empowering individuals through sports have made Nike a global leader in athletic apparel and footwear.

Branding is a powerful force that goes beyond a mere logo or advertising campaign. It encapsulates a company's purpose, values, and visual identity, creating an emotional connection with consumers. Through consistent messaging and an unwavering commitment to their brand essence, businesses can carve their place in the hearts and minds of their target market. So, dare to be bold, purposeful, and authentic, for a well-crafted brand has the potential to leave an indelible mark on the world.

As the world continues to evolve, so too do brands. The digital age has opened up new avenues for brand engagement and storytelling. Social media platforms have become powerful tools for brands to connect directly with their audience, fostering a sense of community and allowing for real-time interactions. Memorable brands adapt and embrace these technological advancements, utilizing them to amplify their message and strengthen their brand identity.

Originally an online bookstore, Amazon has transformed into a global e-commerce powerhouse. The brand's commitment to convenience, fast delivery, and a vast product selection has made it a household name. Through strategic acquisitions and innovative services like Amazon Prime and Amazon Web Services, the company has expanded its reach and disrupted numerous industries.

Airbnb disrupted the hospitality industry by offering a unique platform for individuals to rent out their homes to travelers. By leveraging the power of the sharing economy and providing personalized experiences, Airbnb has redefined travel and accommodations. Their brand has evolved beyond lodging, with experiences and community-driven initiatives, reinforcing their commitment to connection and exploration.

Tesla's brand represents more than just electric vehicles; it signifies innovation, sustainability, and a vision for the future. By pushing the boundaries of electric vehicle technology and creating a strong brand community, Tesla has revolutionized the automotive industry. Its CEO, Elon Musk, has become synonymous with the brand, embodying its entrepreneurial spirit and ambition.

As music consumption shifted towards streaming platforms, Spotify emerged as a leader in the industry. The brand leveraged personalized recommendations, curated playlists, and social sharing features to create a personalized music experience. Spotify successfully positioned itself as a go-to platform for discovering and enjoying music, and it has expanded its offerings to include podcasts and other audio content.

Memorable brands have a profound influence on consumer behavior. A strong brand can create a sense of familiarity, trust, and loyalty, leading consumers to choose a brand over its competitors. Effective branding allows companies to charge premium prices, as consumers perceive added value and quality associated with the brand. Additionally, brands that effectively communicate their purpose and values can attract like-minded consumers who identify with their message, creating a strong sense of brand advocacy and loyalty.

Looking ahead, the power of branding will continue to be instrumental in shaping consumer preferences and driving business success. However, as markets become increasingly saturated and consumer expectations evolve, brands will need to adapt and innovate to stay relevant. Embracing emerging technologies such as artificial intelligence, virtual reality, and immersive experiences will allow brands to create even more impactful and personalized connections with their audience.

The power of branding is undeniable. Memorable brands transcend their products or services, resonating with consumers on a deeper level. By understanding and implementing the core principles of effective branding, businesses can differentiate themselves from the competition and create lasting connections with their target market. As brands evolve and adapt to the changing landscape, the potential to leave a lasting impact on consumers and society as a whole remains stronger than ever.

Behind the success of memorable brands lies a deep understanding of human psychology. Brand recognition, the ability of consumers to identify and recall a brand, is influenced by various psychological factors. In this chapter, we will explore the intricate workings of the human mind and how brands strategically leverage these principles to establish strong recognition and foster brand loyalty.

One of the fundamental psychological drivers behind brand recognition is familiarity. Our brains have a natural tendency to prefer and trust the familiar. This preference stems from the cognitive principle known as the mere-exposure effect. The more we are exposed to something, the more we tend to like and trust it. Memorable brands capitalize on this phenomenon by consistently exposing consumers to their brand elements, including logos, taglines, and brand colors. Through repeated exposure, brands become ingrained in our memory, creating a sense of familiarity and comfort.

Brand recognition is heavily influenced by our perceptions and how we interpret the world around us. Our brains are wired to seek patterns and make associations, which brands cleverly utilize. They carefully craft visual elements and messaging to align with consumers' pre-existing perceptions and cultural associations. By leveraging symbolism, metaphor, and emotional triggers, brands shape how we perceive their offerings. For example, luxury brands use high-end aesthetics and exclusive imagery to create an association with wealth, status, and prestige.

Emotions play a significant role in the recognition and recall of brands. Research has consistently shown that emotional experiences leave a lasting impact on our memory. Memorable brands strategically tap into our emotions, evoking feelings of happiness, joy, excitement, or even nostalgia. By forging an emotional connection with consumers, brands create a deeper level of engagement and loyalty. Coca-Cola's heartwarming holiday commercials, for instance, evoke feelings of warmth, togetherness, and nostalgia, strengthening their brand recognition during the festive season.

Our brains process information in different ways, and brands utilize cognitive processing principles to enhance recognition. Two prominent cognitive processing theories are the dual-coding theory and the schema theory. The dual-coding theory suggests that combining verbal and visual information enhances memory retention. Memorable brands use this by pairing memorable visuals with catchy slogans or jingles, creating a dual-coded memory imprint. The schema theory, on the other hand, emphasizes the importance of pre-existing mental frameworks. Brands align their messaging and visuals with consumers' existing schemas, allowing for easier encoding and recall.

Consistency is a key factor in brand recognition. Brands strive to maintain a consistent image across all touchpoints and communication channels. Consistent use of logos, color schemes, typography, and brand voice creates a cohesive brand identity that is easier to recognize and recall. Moreover, consistent messaging and brand experiences help reinforce the mental associations consumers have with a brand, further solidifying its recognition in their minds.

Brand recognition is a complex interplay of psychological processes. By understanding the psychology behind recognition, brands can strategically create experiences that leave a lasting impact on consumers. Leveraging familiarity, perception, emotion, cognitive processing principles, and consistency, memorable brands establish strong connections with their target audience. Through these psychological strategies, brands create a psychological shorthand that allows consumers to instantly recognize and engage with their offerings, leading to increased brand loyalty and market success.

In today's digital landscape, establishing a strong brand recognition online has become paramount for businesses. With millions of websites, social media platforms, and online advertisements vying for attention, it is crucial to stand out from the digital noise. In this chapter, we will explore why building strong brand recognition online is essential and how it can drive success in the digital realm.

The online world has become a central hub for information, interactions, and commerce. Consumers increasingly turn to the internet to discover, research, and engage with brands. Having a robust online presence allows businesses to meet their target audience where they spend a significant amount of their time. By building strong brand recognition online, companies can enhance visibility, expand their reach, and create meaningful connections with their digital-savvy customers.

Online platforms offer unparalleled opportunities for brand visibility. With search engines, social media, and online advertising, businesses can reach a vast audience quickly and cost-effectively. By strategically optimizing their websites for search engines, utilizing targeted digital advertising, and actively engaging on social media, brands can increase their online visibility and capture the attention of potential customers. Strong brand recognition online ensures that when consumers are looking for relevant products or services, your brand is at the forefront of their minds.

In the digital world, trust is a critical currency. Building strong brand recognition online helps establish trust and credibility with consumers. Through consistent branding, engaging content, and positive online interactions, brands can develop a reputation for reliability, expertise, and authenticity. Online reviews and testimonials from satisfied customers further contribute to building trust. A trusted brand is more likely to attract and retain customers, as people feel confident in their association with a reputable and recognizable brand.

User experience (UX) plays a vital role in building strong brand recognition online. A well-designed website, intuitive navigation, and seamless interactions contribute to a positive and memorable user experience. When users have a seamless and enjoyable experience interacting with a brand online, it increases the likelihood of them returning, engaging, and recommending the brand to others. Brands that prioritize creating a memorable user experience online differentiate themselves from the competition and foster long-term customer loyalty.

Online platforms offer numerous avenues for customer engagement. Brands can leverage social media, email marketing, and interactive website features to engage directly with their audience. By actively participating in conversations, responding to inquiries, and sharing valuable content, brands create a sense of connection and community. Strong brand recognition online encourages customers to engage with the brand, share their experiences, and become brand advocates, amplifying the brand's reach and influence.

In today's digitally driven world, the competition is fierce. Building strong brand recognition online is essential for staying competitive and relevant. Brands that neglect their online presence risk falling behind competitors who actively embrace digital marketing and brand-building strategies. A strong online presence helps brands remain top-of-mind, gain a competitive edge, and adapt to evolving consumer behaviors and preferences in the digital realm.

Building strong brand recognition online is no longer optional but essential for businesses aiming to thrive in the digital age. It offers increased brand visibility, establishes trust and credibility, creates memorable user experiences, drives customer engagement, and keeps businesses competitive in a digital landscape. By investing in a robust online presence, brands can effectively connect with their target audience, foster brand loyalty, and reap the rewards of digital success. Embrace the digital realm, build your brand's recognition online, and position yourself for continued growth and prosperity.

Social media platforms have emerged as powerful tools for building brand recognition online. With billions of active users, platforms like Facebook, Instagram, Twitter, and LinkedIn offer unprecedented opportunities for brands to engage with their audience. By creating compelling content, fostering meaningful conversations, and utilizing targeted advertising, brands can significantly enhance their online visibility and strengthen their brand recognition. The viral nature of social media allows brands to reach a vast audience quickly, amplifying their message and extending their brand's influence.

A strong online brand recognition has a direct impact on conversion and sales. When consumers are familiar with a brand and have positive associations with it, they are more likely to choose that brand over competitors. Online brand recognition helps build trust and credibility, mitigating any doubts or hesitations consumers may have during the purchase decision-making process. Additionally, strong brand recognition can lead to increased brand loyalty, repeat purchases, and referrals, driving long-term business growth and profitability.

As mobile usage continues to rise, brands must adapt to the preferences and behaviors of mobile-first consumers. A robust online presence that is optimized for mobile devices is crucial for building strong brand recognition. Responsive websites, mobile apps, and mobile-friendly content ensure that users have a seamless and engaging experience, regardless of the device they are using. By catering to mobile users, brands can meet their audience where they are and maximize their brand's visibility and recognition.

The digital landscape is dynamic and ever-evolving. Building strong brand recognition online enables brands to stay relevant and engage with their audience in real-time. By actively monitoring trends, participating in online conversations, and creating timely and relevant content, brands can position themselves as thought leaders and stay at the forefront of their industry. Furthermore, leveraging emerging technologies and platforms, such as live streaming, virtual reality, or augmented reality, can provide unique and immersive experiences that captivate audiences and enhance brand recognition.

The digital realm offers unparalleled opportunities for tracking and measuring brand recognition efforts. Brands can utilize analytics tools to monitor website traffic, social media engagement, and conversion rates. These insights provide valuable data for measuring the effectiveness of branding strategies and making informed decisions to optimize future efforts. By analyzing data and adapting strategies based on the results, brands can continually refine their online presence and strengthen their brand recognition over time.

In a digital-first world, building strong brand recognition online is not just important—it is imperative. It enables brands to connect with their target audience, build trust and credibility, drive conversion and sales, adapt to changing consumer behaviors, and stay relevant and engaging in a dynamic digital landscape. By leveraging the power of social media, embracing mobile optimization, and staying abreast of emerging trends, brands can establish a strong online presence that resonates with their audience and sets them apart from the competition. Embrace the digital realm, build your brand's recognition online, and unlock the vast potential for growth and success in the digital age.

The Art of Communication

In the vast tapestry of human existence, few forces hold as much influence as the words we choose to express ourselves. From ancient scrolls to modern-day social media, our words shape opinions, ignite revolutions, and forge connections between individuals. In this chapter, we explore the profound impact that words have on our lives and the world around us, reminding ourselves that every utterance carries weight and meaning.

Imagine a world without words—a barren landscape where thoughts remain trapped within our minds, unable to bridge the gap between souls. Words are the seeds of communication, sprouting into ideas and emotions, nurturing understanding, empathy, and growth. They create a symphony of expression, offering a glimpse into the depths of our being.

Just as a gentle flap of a butterfly's wings can cause a ripple effect across continents, our words possess the power to create waves of change. A single sentence can spark inspiration or incite hatred, uplift spirits or crush dreams. Each word is a brushstroke on the canvas of reality, capable of shaping destinies, toppling empires, or healing broken hearts.

Words can serve as both weapons and shields, capable of inflicting deep wounds or providing solace in times of turmoil. They possess the ability to unite nations or sow seeds of division, to kindle hope or ignite fear. With every syllable, we possess the choice to uplift or tear down, to foster understanding or deepen ignorance. It is our responsibility to wield our words wisely, knowing that their impact can reverberate long after they have been spoken.

Through our words, we can bridge the gaps that separate us, finding common ground amidst our differences. When we choose to listen and speak with empathy, our words become a bridge that connects hearts and minds. They open doors to compassion, encourage dialogue, and foster unity in a world often fragmented by misunderstanding.

Stories are the lifeblood of human existence, passed down through generations to shape our collective consciousness. They inspire, educate, and entertain. Whether told through literature, film, or oral tradition, stories have the power to challenge our perspectives, ignite our imagination, and transform lives. The words we choose in these narratives shape our understanding of ourselves and the world we inhabit.

With great power comes great responsibility. As individuals, we must recognize the weight our words carry and the impact they have on those around us. We can choose to uplift, encourage, and inspire, or we can opt for a path of negativity, criticism, and apathy. Our words can be a catalyst for positive change, offering hope in times of despair and instilling confidence in the hearts of others.

Let us remember that our words extend beyond our immediate surroundings. In an interconnected world, our words can reach far beyond our intended audience, resonating with individuals we may never meet. A single thought expressed eloquently can ripple through social media platforms, reaching corners of the globe we may have never thought possible. We must be mindful of the potential impact of our words and strive to be a force for good in a world that craves understanding and compassion.

Words are not mere combinations of letters and sounds; they are the building blocks of our thoughts, emotions, and connections. They possess the power to shape narratives, redefine paradigms, and transform lives. Let us recognize the immense responsibility that lies within our hands as we navigate the intricacies of human expression.

Communication is the lifeblood of success. Whether in personal relationships, professional endeavors, or societal interactions, the ability to communicate effectively can propel us toward our goals, foster collaboration, and inspire others to join us on our journey. In this chapter, we explore the various facets of communication and how it can be leveraged to unlock success in every aspect of our lives.

Effective communication is the key that unlocks the door to meaningful connections. By expressing ourselves clearly and genuinely, we build trust, establish rapport, and create bonds with others. Successful communicators understand the importance of active listening, empathy, and nonverbal cues, allowing them to forge connections that transcend superficial interactions.

Communication is a powerful tool for persuasion. Whether we're seeking to inspire, motivate, or influence others, the ability to articulate our ideas persuasively can sway opinions and drive change. By mastering the art of persuasion, we can mobilize support, build alliances, and rally others around a shared vision, propelling us closer to our goals.

Effective communication is the cornerstone of healthy relationships. Whether in personal or professional settings, the ability to express our needs, concerns, and aspirations fosters understanding, trust, and respect. By cultivating open lines of communication, we create an environment that nurtures collaboration, teamwork, and long-term success.

In a world increasingly interconnected, effective communication enables us to bridge cultural, linguistic, and ideological divides. By embracing diversity and seeking to understand different perspectives, we can transcend barriers, foster inclusivity, and cultivate global networks. Successful communicators recognize the value of cross-cultural understanding and leverage it to build bridges that span continents.

Leadership and effective communication go hand in hand. A skilled leader understands the power of clear and inspiring communication to motivate, guide, and inspire their team. By communicating a compelling vision, providing feedback, and fostering a culture of open dialogue, leaders empower their teams to achieve remarkable feats and drive organizational success.

Effective communication is particularly crucial in times of conflict and challenge. It enables us to navigate difficult conversations, resolve disputes, and find common ground. By employing active listening, empathy, and diplomacy, we can defuse tense situations, foster understanding, and arrive at mutually beneficial solutions.

In today's digital era, communication has taken on new dimensions. Social media, email, and instant messaging have revolutionized the way we connect with others. Successful communicators adapt to this changing landscape, leveraging technology to disseminate ideas, amplify their message, and reach wider audiences. They understand the nuances of digital communication, recognizing the importance of clarity, brevity, and responsible online engagement.

Effective communication is a skill that can be honed and leveraged to unlock success in every sphere of life. By mastering the art of connection, persuasion, and relationship-building, we can forge meaningful connections, inspire others, and overcome challenges. In a world where ideas are exchanged at lightning speed, those who can communicate with clarity, empathy, and authenticity hold the keys to success. Let us embrace the power of effective communication and harness its potential to shape our lives and the world around us.

Successful communication is not just about expressing ourselves; it is equally important to be an active listener. Active listening involves giving our undivided attention, seeking to understand, and responding thoughtfully. When we genuinely listen to others, we create an environment of respect and trust. By acknowledging their perspectives, validating their emotions, and responding empathetically, we build stronger relationships and create opportunities for collaboration and success.

In a world filled with information overload, the ability to communicate clearly and concisely is a valuable skill. Being able to distill complex ideas into simple and understandable terms allows us to convey our message effectively. Clear communication eliminates confusion, reduces misunderstandings, and ensures that our intended meaning is received accurately. Whether it's delivering a presentation, writing an email, or engaging in conversation, the art of brevity and clarity enhances our chances of success.

Effective communicators understand the importance of tailoring their message to suit different audiences. Not everyone communicates or comprehends information in the same way. By adapting our communication style, language, and delivery to resonate with our specific audience, we can maximize our impact. Whether it's speaking to a diverse team, addressing a group of stakeholders, or engaging with customers, the ability to adapt ensures that our message is received and understood by those we seek to influence.

Communication, like any skill, can be honed and improved upon with practice. Successful communicators are committed to ongoing self-improvement. They seek feedback, reflect on their communication style, and make adjustments as necessary. Whether through public speaking courses, workshops on effective writing, or interpersonal communication training, they invest in their own development to become more effective communicators. This commitment to growth ensures that they remain adaptable and relevant in an ever-evolving world.

Success is not achieved in isolation but through collaboration and teamwork. A positive communication culture within teams and organizations is crucial for achieving shared goals. Successful communicators foster an environment where open dialogue, constructive feedback, and diverse perspectives are encouraged. They create space for everyone to contribute and ensure that communication channels are transparent and accessible. By promoting a culture of respect, trust, and inclusivity, they unleash the collective potential of their teams and drive them towards success.

Communication is a multifaceted tool that can be leveraged for success in all areas of life. By embracing active listening, clarity, adaptability, and continuous improvement, we can enhance our ability to connect, influence, and collaborate with others. Effective communication transcends boundaries, bridges gaps, and creates opportunities. It is the foundation upon which we build strong relationships, inspire action, and achieve our goals. Let us recognize the power of communication and commit to mastering this invaluable skill, knowing that it holds the key to unlocking our full potential.

In the digital age, online communication has become an indispensable tool for businesses. The ability to effectively communicate and connect with customers, clients, and partners through various online channels can significantly impact the success of an online business. In this chapter, we explore strategies for harnessing the art of online communication to achieve success in the ever-evolving world of e-commerce and digital entrepreneurship.

In the online world, your business's digital presence is often the first point of contact for potential customers. Creating a compelling online presence requires strategic communication. Through your website, social media profiles, and online content, convey your brand's identity, values, and unique selling proposition clearly and consistently. Engage your audience with compelling visuals, captivating storytelling, and concise messaging that resonates with your target market.

Online communication allows you to build authentic connections with your audience. Engage in conversations, respond to comments and messages, and foster a sense of community around your brand. By being genuine, approachable, and responsive, you establish trust and loyalty, which are crucial for business success. Use online platforms to showcase your expertise, provide valuable content, and create opportunities for meaningful interactions with your audience.

Email marketing remains a powerful tool for online businesses. Craft compelling and personalized email campaigns that resonate with your subscribers. Segment your email list to ensure that your messages are relevant and tailored to each group's interests and needs. Utilize persuasive copywriting techniques, compelling subject lines, and clear call-to-actions to drive engagement and conversions. Regularly analyze email metrics to refine your approach and optimize your results.

Social media platforms are invaluable for online businesses to reach and engage with their target audience. Identify the platforms where your target market is most active, and develop a social media strategy that aligns with your brand voice and objectives. Create and curate engaging content, encourage conversations, and build relationships with your followers. Utilize social media analytics to track performance, identify trends, and refine your approach for maximum impact.

Influencer marketing has become a popular strategy for online businesses to expand their reach and build credibility. Identify influencers whose audience aligns with your target market and collaborate on authentic partnerships. Develop clear communication and expectations, ensuring that the influencer effectively communicates your brand's message to their audience. Monitor and measure the impact of these collaborations to assess their effectiveness.

Online businesses must prioritize effective communication when it comes to customer support. Establish multiple channels for customers to reach out, such as live chat, email, or social media messaging. Respond promptly, professionally, and empathetically to customer inquiries, concerns, and feedback. By providing exceptional customer service, you foster loyalty, encourage positive reviews, and generate word-of-mouth referrals.

Online communication enables businesses to collaborate with partners, affiliates, and other industry professionals seamlessly. Engage in joint ventures, guest blogging, webinars, and online events to expand your network and reach new audiences. By leveraging online collaboration, you tap into the collective expertise and resources of others, amplifying your business's visibility and credibility.

Online communication is a powerful asset for businesses operating in the digital landscape. By crafting a compelling online presence, building authentic connections, utilizing email marketing and social media effectively, leveraging influencer partnerships, providing exceptional customer support, and embracing online collaboration, you can harness the art of online communication to achieve success in your online business. Continuously adapt your communication strategies to stay relevant in the rapidly evolving online marketplace and embrace emerging technologies and platforms to unlock new opportunities for growth. Remember, effective online communication can be the difference between mediocrity and outstanding success in the online business realm. Embrace the art of online communication as a strategic tool, one that allows you to connect, engage, and build relationships with your target audience.

As you embark on your online business journey, remember these key principles:

Consistency and authenticity are crucial elements of effective online communication. Maintain a consistent brand voice, visual identity, and messaging across all online channels. Be authentic in your interactions, showcasing the genuine values and personality of your business. Online audiences appreciate transparency and honesty, so avoid overly promotional or misleading tactics. By staying true to your brand and consistently delivering value, you build trust and credibility over time.

In the digital realm, visual content reigns supreme. Leverage the power of visuals to capture attention and communicate your message effectively. Utilize high-quality images, videos, infographics, and other visual elements that align with your brand aesthetic. Visual communication is more likely to engage and resonate with your audience, driving higher levels of interaction and sharing across online platforms.

In the online world, data is king. Leverage data and analytics tools to gather insights into your online communication efforts. Monitor key performance indicators such as website traffic, engagement metrics, conversion rates, and customer feedback. Analyze the data to identify trends, optimize your communication strategies, and make data-driven decisions. Continuously experiment, refine, and adapt your approach based on the insights gained from data analysis.

In a crowded online marketplace, personalization is a key differentiator. Tailor your communication to individual customers whenever possible. Use data to segment your audience and deliver personalized content, recommendations, and offers. Address customers by name, provide relevant product suggestions, and personalize your email marketing campaigns. By making your customers feel seen and understood, you deepen their connection with your brand and foster loyalty.

The online business landscape is ever-evolving, with new technologies, platforms, and communication trends emerging constantly. Stay agile and adaptable, willing to experiment with new communication channels and strategies. Stay informed about the latest trends, such as live video streaming, chatbots, voice search, and social media innovations. Embrace change and be open to adopting new tools and techniques that can enhance your online communication and keep your business ahead of the curve.

In the digital era, effective online communication is an essential element of achieving success in the world of online business. By embracing consistency, authenticity, visual communication, data-driven decision-making, personalization, and adaptability, you can leverage the art of online communication to propel your business to new heights. Remember that the online realm offers boundless opportunities for connection and growth, so approach your communication strategies with creativity, intention, and a focus on building meaningful relationships with your audience.

One of the remarkable aspects of online business is the ability to create and nurture a vibrant community around your brand. Cultivate an engaged online community by fostering conversations, encouraging user-generated content, and creating spaces for customers to connect with each other. Through forums, social media groups, and interactive platforms, facilitate discussions, provide valuable resources, and seek feedback from your community. A strong online community not only fosters brand loyalty but also serves as a valuable source of insights and feedback to help you improve your products and services.

Content marketing is a powerful tool for online businesses to attract, engage, and retain customers. Create high-quality and relevant content that aligns with the interests and needs of your target audience. Develop a content strategy that incorporates blog posts, articles, videos, podcasts, and other formats that resonate with your audience. Optimize your content for search engines to increase visibility and drive organic traffic to your website. Share your expertise, provide valuable insights, and establish yourself as a trusted authority in your industry through compelling and informative content.

Collaborating with influencers and affiliates can significantly amplify your online business's reach and credibility. Identify influencers or affiliates whose audience aligns with your target market and form partnerships that are mutually beneficial. Work with influencers to create authentic content that promotes your products or services. Offer affiliate programs to incentivize partners to promote your business. Leverage the influence and reach of these individuals to expand your customer base and generate sales.

In the fast-paced online world, it is crucial to actively listen and engage with your audience. Monitor social media platforms, online forums, and review sites to gather feedback and insights about your brand. Respond promptly and thoughtfully to customer comments, inquiries, and concerns. Show appreciation for positive feedback and address any negative feedback or complaints with empathy and a solution-oriented mindset. By actively engaging with your audience, you demonstrate your commitment to customer satisfaction and build a reputation for exceptional customer service.

Online advertising allows you to reach a targeted audience and drive traffic to your website or online store. Utilize platforms like Google Ads, social media advertising, and display advertising to reach potential customers. Develop compelling ad copy, captivating visuals, and clear calls-to-action to maximize the impact of your ads. Continuously monitor and optimize your online advertising campaigns to ensure they align with your business objectives and deliver a strong return on investment.

In the realm of online business, harnessing the art of online communication is vital for achieving success. By building a strong online community, leveraging content marketing, utilizing influencer and affiliate partnerships, actively listening and engaging with your audience, and harnessing the power of online advertising, you can propel your online business to new heights. Embrace the ever-changing digital landscape, adapt to emerging technologies and trends, and continue to refine your online communication strategies. With dedication, creativity, and a customer-centric approach, your online business can thrive and achieve remarkable success in the vast online marketplace.

The Digital Marketplace

Over the past few decades, the internet has transformed the way we live, work, and connect with one another. One of its most significant contributions is its role as a bustling marketplace, where buyers and sellers from all corners of the globe come together to exchange goods, services, and ideas. In this chapter, we will explore how the internet has evolved into a vibrant digital marketplace, revolutionizing commerce and creating boundless opportunities for individuals and businesses alike.

The inception of the internet marked a turning point in the way we engage in trade and commerce. Traditional brick-and-mortar stores and physical marketplaces have now been supplemented, and in some cases, even replaced by online platforms. This shift gave birth to e-commerce, an industry that has grown exponentially over the years. E-commerce platforms offer the convenience of shopping from the comfort of your home, allowing customers to browse through an extensive range of products and make purchases with just a few clicks.

One of the most remarkable aspects of the internet as a digital marketplace is its global reach. Geographical boundaries no longer pose a significant barrier to trade. Sellers can now showcase their products to a worldwide audience, and buyers can access a vast array of offerings from every corner of the globe. This newfound accessibility has not only expanded market opportunities for businesses but has also provided consumers with an unprecedented level of choice and variety.

To facilitate the buying and selling process, numerous online marketplace platforms have emerged. These platforms act as intermediaries, connecting buyers and sellers and providing a secure and efficient environment for transactions to take place. Some of the most prominent examples include Amazon, eBay, Alibaba, and Etsy. These platforms offer a wide range of products across diverse categories, allowing businesses of all sizes to establish an online presence and reach a broader customer base.

The internet's digital marketplace has empowered consumers in ways previously unimaginable. Today, buyers can research products, compare prices, read reviews, and gather information before making a purchase decision. This wealth of knowledge at their fingertips enables consumers to make informed choices and find the best deals available. Furthermore, the ability to leave reviews and ratings on products allows shoppers to contribute to the collective knowledge of the marketplace, fostering transparency and accountability.

The digital marketplace has leveled the playing field for small businesses and entrepreneurs. In the past, establishing a physical store and reaching a wide customer base required significant resources. However, with the advent of the internet, anyone with an internet connection can set up an online store and showcase their products to a global audience. This has opened up immense opportunities for individuals to turn their passions into profitable ventures, creating a thriving ecosystem of startups and small-scale enterprises.

While the internet's digital marketplace presents remarkable opportunities, it is not without its challenges. Competition in the online space can be fierce, requiring businesses to adopt effective marketing strategies and provide exceptional customer experiences. Cybersecurity threats and online scams also pose risks to both buyers and sellers, highlighting the importance of vigilance and online safety practices.

The internet has transformed into a dynamic and bustling digital marketplace, redefining the way we buy and sell goods and services. From the convenience of e-commerce to the global reach of online marketplaces, the internet has revolutionized commerce and provided unparalleled opportunities for businesses and consumers alike. As technology continues to advance, the digital marketplace will undoubtedly evolve, promising an exciting future of innovation and growth for all those involved.

With the vastness of the digital marketplace, it is essential to understand how to navigate its intricacies effectively. Here are some key considerations to keep in mind:

Before engaging in any online transactions, it is crucial to conduct thorough research and due diligence. This includes verifying the credibility of sellers, reading customer reviews, and checking for any potential red flags. Being well-informed about the product, its quality, and the reputation of the seller will help ensure a satisfactory buying experience.

When making purchases online, it is essential to prioritize security. Reputable online marketplaces employ secure payment gateways to protect your financial information. However, it is also advisable to take personal precautions, such as using secure payment methods like credit cards or trusted third-party services like PayPal. Avoid sharing sensitive information through unsecured channels or unfamiliar websites.

Before making a purchase, carefully review the terms and conditions set by the online marketplace and the seller. Pay attention to details such as shipping and return policies, warranty information, and dispute resolution processes. Being aware of these aspects will help you navigate potential challenges or conflicts that may arise during the buying process.

Established online marketplaces often provide reliable customer support services. If you encounter any issues or have questions regarding a purchase, don't hesitate to reach out to their customer support team for assistance. Clear and prompt communication with the seller or marketplace will help resolve any concerns and ensure a positive experience.

Safeguarding your personal information is vital when engaging in online transactions. Be cautious about sharing unnecessary personal details and ensure that the websites you interact with have proper security measures in place. Regularly update your passwords, use two-factor authentication whenever possible, and be cautious of phishing attempts or suspicious emails.

The digital marketplace thrives on user feedback and reviews. As a consumer, you can contribute to this ecosystem by leaving reviews and ratings for products and sellers you have engaged with. Similarly, take advantage of others' experiences by reading reviews before making a purchase. This collaborative approach helps maintain transparency, build trust, and foster a healthy online marketplace.

The internet's transformation into a digital marketplace has revolutionized the way we buy and sell products and services. With its global reach, diverse offerings, and opportunities for both established businesses and aspiring entrepreneurs, the digital marketplace continues to shape the future of commerce.

By understanding the dynamics of the digital marketplace, conducting thorough research, prioritizing security, and leveraging user feedback, you can navigate this vast landscape with confidence. As you embark on your online buying and selling journey, remember to adapt to the evolving nature of the digital marketplace, stay informed about emerging trends, and embrace the boundless possibilities it presents.

The internet has transformed the way we communicate and conduct business, enabling connections and transactions on a global scale. By taking your product online, you gain access to a vast pool of potential customers who may be interested in what you have to offer. The worldwide customer base represents diverse cultures, backgrounds, and preferences, creating a vibrant marketplace that can lead to significant growth and success.

Unlike traditional brick-and-mortar stores, which are confined to a specific location, an online presence allows you to transcend geographical boundaries. With the right marketing strategies and a compelling online presence, your product can reach customers in different countries, continents, and time zones. This opens up a world of possibilities, as you can tap into emerging markets and cater to niche audiences that may have a strong demand for your product.

Expanding your customer base globally requires an understanding of different cultures and their preferences. What appeals to customers in one country may not resonate with those in another. Take the time to research and adapt your marketing strategies, product presentation, and messaging to suit the cultural nuances of your target audience. By demonstrating cultural sensitivity and localization efforts, you can establish stronger connections with customers worldwide.

Language plays a crucial role in effectively reaching and engaging with a worldwide customer base. While English is widely spoken, translating your product descriptions, website content, and customer support into other languages can significantly enhance your reach and customer satisfaction. Partnering with professional translation services or using machine translation tools can help you overcome language barriers and create a more inclusive and personalized experience for customers in different regions.

Selling your product worldwide involves addressing logistical challenges, such as international shipping and customs regulations. Research reputable shipping companies that offer reliable international services and consider partnering with fulfillment centers or third-party logistics providers to streamline your shipping processes. Ensure that you have a clear understanding of import/export requirements, taxes, and duties specific to each target market to avoid any delays or complications.

To cater to a global customer base, it is important to offer diverse payment options that align with the preferences of different regions. While credit cards are commonly used worldwide, consider integrating alternative payment methods that are popular in specific countries or regions, such as digital wallets, bank transfers, or local payment gateways. This flexibility will improve the buying experience and remove any barriers to purchasing your product.

Trust is paramount when selling to a worldwide customer base. Invest in building a strong online presence through a well-designed website, engaging content, and social media presence. Display customer reviews and testimonials to instill confidence in potential buyers. Establish clear channels for customer support, and be responsive to inquiries and concerns, regardless of the customer's location. Proactively addressing customer needs will strengthen your reputation and foster long-term relationships.

Embracing a worldwide customer base by selling your product online opens up vast opportunities for growth and success. By leveraging the power of global connectivity, breaking down geographical barriers, and understanding cultural nuances, you can effectively tap into diverse markets and reach customers worldwide. Remember to adapt your marketing strategies, embrace language localization, address logistical considerations, and prioritize

You have decided to embark on an exciting journey of selling your product online. One of the most compelling aspects of the digital marketplace is the potential to reach a worldwide customer base. The internet has bridged geographical barriers, allowing businesses like yours to connect with customers from all corners of the globe. In this chapter, we will explore the vast opportunities that await you in reaching an international audience and provide guidance on how to effectively tap into this global market.

The internet has transformed the way we communicate and conduct business, enabling connections and transactions on a global scale. By taking your product online, you gain access to a vast pool of potential customers who may be interested in what you have to offer. The worldwide customer base represents diverse cultures, backgrounds, and preferences, creating a vibrant marketplace that can lead to significant growth and success.

Unlike traditional brick-and-mortar stores, which are confined to a specific location, an online presence allows you to transcend geographical boundaries. With the right marketing strategies and a compelling online presence, your product can reach customers in different countries, continents, and time zones. This opens up a world of possibilities, as you can tap into emerging markets and cater to niche audiences that may have a strong demand for your product.

Expanding your customer base globally requires an understanding of different cultures and their preferences. What appeals to customers in one country may not resonate with those in another. Take the time to research and adapt your marketing strategies, product presentation, and messaging to suit the cultural nuances of your target audience. By demonstrating cultural sensitivity and localization efforts, you can establish stronger connections with customers worldwide.

Language plays a crucial role in effectively reaching and engaging with a worldwide customer base. While English is widely spoken, translating your product descriptions, website content, and customer support into other languages can significantly enhance your reach and customer satisfaction. Partnering with professional translation services or using machine translation tools can help you overcome language barriers and create a more inclusive and personalized experience for customers in different regions.

Selling your product worldwide involves addressing logistical challenges, such as international shipping and customs regulations. Research reputable shipping companies that offer reliable international services and consider partnering with fulfillment centers or third-party logistics providers to streamline your shipping processes. Ensure that you have a clear understanding of import/export requirements, taxes, and duties specific to each target market to avoid any delays or complications.

To cater to a global customer base, it is important to offer diverse payment options that align with the preferences of different regions. While credit cards are commonly used worldwide, consider integrating alternative payment methods that are popular in specific countries or regions, such as digital wallets, bank transfers, or local payment gateways. This flexibility will improve the buying experience and remove any barriers to purchasing your product.

Trust is paramount when selling to a worldwide customer base. Invest in building a strong online presence through a well-designed website, engaging content, and social media presence. Display customer reviews and testimonials to instill confidence in potential buyers. Establish clear channels for customer support, and be responsive to inquiries and concerns, regardless of the customer's location. Proactively addressing customer needs will strengthen your reputation and foster long-term relationships.

The global online marketplace continues to expand at a rapid pace, offering tremendous growth opportunities for businesses that venture beyond their domestic markets. Consider the following statistics:

According to eMarketer, global retail e-commerce sales are projected to reach $6.54 trillion by 2023, demonstrating the immense potential of selling products online to a worldwide customer base.

The Asia-Pacific region, specifically China, has emerged as a dominant force in e-commerce. In 2020, China accounted for 52.1% of global retail e-commerce sales, according to Statista. This showcases the substantial market opportunities that exist in this region.

Cross-border e-commerce is also on the rise. A study by eShopWorld reveals that 70% of online shoppers have made purchases from international retailers. This demonstrates the willingness of customers to explore and buy products from overseas sellers.

Marketplaces like Amazon, eBay, and Alibaba have witnessed exponential growth in their user base and sales figures. For instance, Amazon reported net sales of $386 billion in 2020, showcasing the vast potential of selling on global platforms.

Social media platforms have also become influential in driving online sales. According to Hootsuite and We Are Social, around 4.2 billion people worldwide use social media, offering a vast audience for businesses to showcase and sell their products.

The worldwide customer base for your product is waiting to be tapped into through online selling. The power of global connectivity, breaking down geographical barriers, cultural considerations, language localization, and other key strategies can help you effectively reach customers from different regions.

By investing in building trust, providing excellent customer support, and understanding the growth potential of the global online marketplace, you can position your business for success. Stay abreast of market trends, leverage data and insights, and continuously refine your strategies to adapt to the evolving needs and preferences of your international customers.

Remember, the internet has made it possible for businesses of all sizes to expand beyond local markets and access a global customer base. Embrace this opportunity, and with dedication, innovation, and a customer-centric approach, your product can thrive on the worldwide digital stage.

"Education is not the filling of a pail, but the lighting of a fire." - William Butler Yeats

In the grand tapestry of life, there exists a precious thread that can weave wonders into your existence: the thirst for knowledge. It is this insatiable curiosity that has driven humanity forward, shaping our world and enabling progress. As you embark on your own journey, I implore you to cultivate an unwavering commitment to lifelong learning. Open your heart and mind to the vast opportunities that lie ahead, for it is through learning that you will uncover the true depth of your potential.

Imagine a field where seeds are continuously sown, nurtured, and transformed into blooming flowers. Similarly, your mind holds the potential to blossom and grow with every new piece of knowledge you acquire. Adopting a growth mindset means believing in your capacity for growth and improvement. Understand that your abilities are not fixed, but rather malleable, and that through dedication and effort, you can continuously expand your horizons. Embrace challenges as opportunities for growth, and see failures as stepping stones toward success. With this mindset, you will be open to new ideas and unafraid of venturing into uncharted territories.

Learning is not confined to the walls of a classroom or the pages of a textbook. The world around you is a rich tapestry of knowledge waiting to be discovered. Step out of your comfort zone, explore different cultures, engage in conversations with people from various backgrounds, and expose yourself to diverse perspectives. Visit museums, attend lectures, participate in workshops, and immerse yourself in the wonders of nature. By doing so, you will open doors to a multitude of insights and experiences that will broaden your understanding of the world.

In the pursuit of knowledge, there will inevitably be moments of failure and setbacks. Instead of allowing these moments to deter you, view them as valuable learning experiences. Each stumble or setback carries valuable lessons that can propel you forward. Embrace the discomfort of failure, analyze your mistakes, and adjust your course of action accordingly. Remember, even the greatest minds of history faced countless failures before reaching their breakthroughs. Let failure become the stepping stone that leads you to greater heights.

Curiosity is the fuel that ignites the fire of learning. Maintain a childlike wonder about the world and nurture your innate curiosity. Challenge assumptions, question the status quo, and never be afraid to ask questions. Curiosity stimulates critical thinking, drives innovation, and opens doors to unexplored realms of knowledge. As Albert Einstein once said, "I have no special talent. I am only passionately curious." Let your curiosity guide you towards a deeper understanding of yourself and the world around you.

In this digital era, technology has revolutionized the way we access information and learn. Embrace the digital landscape and leverage the power of technology to expand your knowledge. Online courses, educational platforms, podcasts, and interactive learning tools are just a few examples of the vast resources available at your fingertips. Seize the opportunity to learn at your own pace, connect with like-minded individuals, and explore topics that captivate your interest.

One of the most effective ways to solidify your own understanding is by teaching others. As you accumulate knowledge and skills, seek opportunities to share what you have learned with those around you. Mentorship, tutoring, or even contributing to online communities can not only deepen your own understanding but also inspire and empower others on their own learning journeys.

Amidst the constant influx of information, it is crucial to pause, reflect, and assimilate what you have learned. Take the time to review and internalize new concepts, connect them with existing knowledge, and identify areas for further exploration. Engage in journaling, meditation, or discussions with peers to deepen your understanding and gain new insights. Reflection acts as a bridge between learning and application, helping you make meaningful connections and uncover the underlying principles that govern the world.

In the pursuit of knowledge, it is important to remain humble. Recognize that no matter how much you learn, there will always be more to discover. Embrace the vastness of the unknown and approach each learning opportunity with an open mind and a willingness to learn from others. Surround yourself with individuals who challenge and inspire you, and be receptive to their ideas and perspectives. By humbling yourself, you create an environment that fosters continuous growth and learning.

The world is in a constant state of flux, and knowledge evolves alongside it. Embrace the inevitability of change and remain adaptable in your approach to learning. Be open to new ideas, emerging technologies, and evolving paradigms. Embrace the discomfort of stepping out of your comfort zone and embrace the unknown. By doing so, you will not only stay relevant in a rapidly changing world but also unlock new opportunities for personal and professional growth.

Above all, never forget the sheer joy and fulfillment that comes from learning. Learning is not just a means to an end but a lifelong journey that brings excitement, wonder, and growth. Cultivate a genuine passion for knowledge and approach each learning opportunity with enthusiasm. Celebrate your progress, acknowledge your achievements, and revel in the joy of expanding your understanding of the world. Learning is not a chore; it is a privilege that enriches your life in countless ways.

As you navigate the uncharted waters of life, remember that learning is a continuous process. Embrace it wholeheartedly, for it will shape your perspectives, ignite your passions, and lead you to unforeseen opportunities. Stay open to new experiences, seek knowledge in diverse places, and never cease to ask questions. Let the flames of curiosity burn bright within you, guiding you towards a lifetime of growth, discovery, and fulfillment.

Failure is an integral part of the learning process. Instead of fearing failure, embrace it as a catalyst for growth and development. When you encounter setbacks or make mistakes, view them as valuable lessons rather than reasons to give up. Analyze what went wrong, identify areas for improvement, and use that knowledge to refine your approach. Remember, some of the greatest inventions and achievements in history were born out of multiple failures. Embrace failure as a stepping stone on your path to success.

While it is important to specialize in a particular field, don't limit yourself to a narrow scope of knowledge. Embrace interdisciplinary learning by exploring various subjects and disciplines. Seek connections between seemingly unrelated fields and discover how they can complement and enrich one another. The intersection of different disciplines often leads to groundbreaking ideas and innovative solutions. Embracing interdisciplinary learning will expand your perspective, foster creativity, and equip you with a well-rounded understanding of the world.

Learning is not just an external process but also an internal journey of self-discovery. Regularly engage in self-reflection to gain deeper insights into your strengths, weaknesses, and areas for personal growth. Take time to assess your learning goals, evaluate your progress, and adjust your strategies as needed. Self-reflection will help you align your learning endeavors with your values and aspirations, ensuring that your pursuit of knowledge remains purposeful and fulfilling.

Learning does not occur in isolation. Embrace the power of collaboration and networking to enhance your learning experience. Engage in meaningful discussions, join study groups, participate in workshops, and connect with individuals who share your passion for learning. Collaborative learning exposes you to different perspectives, promotes intellectual exchange, and accelerates your growth. By actively seeking out opportunities for collaboration, you create a supportive and inspiring environment that fuels your learning journey.

While it is important to be open to new knowledge, it is equally crucial to find a balance in your learning pursuits. Avoid overwhelming yourself with an incessant thirst for knowledge that leads to burnout. Embrace a balanced approach by setting realistic goals, prioritizing your learning objectives, and allowing yourself time for rest and rejuvenation. Remember that learning is a lifelong endeavor, and pacing yourself ensures a sustainable and enjoyable journey.

As you accumulate knowledge, do not hoard it to yourself. Embrace the joy of teaching others and sharing your expertise. Teaching not only reinforces your own understanding but also enables you to make a positive impact on others' lives. Whether it's mentoring a colleague, volunteering in your community, or creating educational content, embrace the opportunity to pass on your knowledge and inspire others on their own learning journeys.

By always being open to learning, you embark on a remarkable adventure that transcends boundaries and propels you toward personal and intellectual growth. Embrace the joy of discovery, embrace the challenges, and embrace the transformative power of knowledge. As you navigate the ever-changing world, let learning be your compass, guiding you to a life of fulfillment, wisdom, and endless possibilities.

"The internet is becoming the town square for the global village of tomorrow." - Bill Gates

In today's digital age, the internet has transformed the way businesses operate and connect with their customers. It has opened up a world of opportunities for aspiring entrepreneurs and created a platform for building successful online businesses. Harnessing the internet's insights can be the key to unlocking your business's full potential. In this chapter, we will explore strategies to leverage the internet's vast resources and maximize your chances of success in the online business realm.

To succeed in the online business arena, it is essential to embrace the digital landscape fully. Understand the various online platforms available and choose the ones that align with your business goals and target audience. From social media networks to e-commerce platforms, blogs to online marketplaces, each platform offers unique advantages for building your brand and reaching your target market. Embrace the digital tools and technologies that can streamline your operations, enhance customer experiences, and drive growth.

To effectively harness the internet's insights, you must have a deep understanding of your target audience. Conduct thorough market research to identify your ideal customer profile, their needs, preferences, and online behaviors. Utilize analytics tools and social listening techniques to gather insights into customer sentiment and behavior patterns. This knowledge will enable you to tailor your online business strategies, develop compelling content, and deliver personalized experiences that resonate with your audience.

Establishing a strong online presence is vital for the success of your online business. Create a professional website that showcases your brand, products, and services. Optimize it for search engines to increase visibility and attract organic traffic. Leverage content marketing strategies, such as blogging and video production, to provide valuable information and engage with your audience. Develop a consistent brand voice across all online channels to build trust and brand recognition. Engage in social media marketing to connect with your target audience, foster relationships, and promote your offerings.

SEO plays a crucial role in driving organic traffic to your online business. Invest in understanding the principles of SEO and implement strategies to optimize your website for search engines. Conduct keyword research to identify relevant search terms and incorporate them into your website's content. Develop a solid backlink strategy to increase your website's authority and visibility. Regularly monitor and analyze your website's performance using analytics tools to refine your SEO strategies and stay ahead of the competition.

Content is king in the online world, and a well-executed content marketing strategy can fuel the success of your online business. Create high-quality, valuable content that aligns with your audience's interests and needs. Develop a content calendar to ensure consistency and variety in your content delivery. Leverage different content formats such as blog posts, videos, infographics, podcasts, and social media posts to cater to different preferences and increase engagement. Distribute your content through various channels to maximize its reach and visibility.

Social media platforms offer immense opportunities for building brand awareness, driving traffic, and fostering customer engagement. Identify the social media platforms that are most relevant to your target audience and develop a comprehensive social media marketing strategy. Create compelling and shareable content tailored to each platform. Engage with your audience, respond to their queries, and encourage user-generated content. Leverage paid advertising options to expand your reach and target specific demographics. Monitor and analyze your social media performance to optimize your strategies and capitalize on emerging trends.

The internet provides an abundance of data that can inform your business decisions. Embrace data-driven decision making by leveraging analytics tools and insights from the internet. Track and measure key performance indicators (KPIs) such as website traffic, conversion rates, customer engagement, and social media metrics. Analyze the data to identify trends, patterns, and areas of improvement. Use this information to refine your online business strategies, optimize marketing campaigns, and make data-backed decisions that drive success. Regularly review and update your data analysis processes to stay ahead of evolving market dynamics.

Online communities and influencers can play a significant role in building brand awareness and credibility for your online business. Identify relevant communities and forums where your target audience congregates. Engage in meaningful discussions, provide valuable insights, and establish yourself as an authority in your niche. Collaborate with influencers and thought leaders who have a strong online presence and a loyal following. Partnering with them can expand your reach, enhance your brand's visibility, and drive qualified traffic to your online business.

The internet empowers customers to share their opinions and experiences about products and services. Embrace customer feedback and reviews as a valuable source of insights for your online business. Encourage customers to leave reviews and testimonials on your website and review platforms. Respond promptly and graciously to both positive and negative feedback. Use customer feedback to improve your offerings, enhance customer experiences, and build a strong reputation for your online business.

The internet is a vast and ever-evolving landscape. To stay ahead of the curve and maintain a competitive edge, embrace continuous learning. Stay updated with the latest trends, technologies, and industry best practices through online courses, webinars, podcasts, and industry forums. Engage in networking opportunities to learn from fellow entrepreneurs and industry experts. Continuously adapt and refine your online business strategies based on new insights and emerging opportunities.

Harnessing the internet's insights to build success with your online business requires a strategic and proactive approach. By leveraging the power of digital platforms, understanding your target audience, and staying informed with data-driven decision making, you can position your online business for growth and achieve long-term success. Embrace the boundless opportunities that the internet offers, and let it be the catalyst for your online business's triumph in the digital realm.

Collaborating in the Online World

In the journey towards success, we often find ourselves captivated by tales of individual triumphs and exceptional accomplishments. We idolize the lone genius, the solitary explorer, and the self-made mogul. However, behind many of these stories lies a crucial element that often goes unnoticed—the power of partnership. Throughout history, numerous achievements have been made possible through the collaboration, support, and synergy that arise from working together towards a common goal. In this chapter, we will explore the profound impact of partnerships and how they enable us to reach new heights and achieve extraordinary success.

Partnerships allow individuals to pool their unique strengths, talents, and expertise. By joining forces, we create a dynamic combination that is greater than the sum of its parts. Consider the world of business, where partnerships between visionary leaders and skilled executives have resulted in groundbreaking innovations and game-changing strategies. Through collaboration, diverse perspectives and skills merge, enabling us to tackle complex challenges with greater efficiency and effectiveness. Together, we can bridge gaps in knowledge, fill skillset voids, and create well-rounded teams that excel in their respective fields.

No individual possesses all the knowledge required to excel in every aspect of life. Partnerships offer the opportunity to tap into a vast pool of knowledge, experiences, and perspectives. When we come together, we can learn from one another, share ideas, and broaden our horizons. This exchange of knowledge fuels innovation, drives growth, and propels us forward. By embracing partnerships, we open ourselves to new possibilities and expand our understanding of the world, ultimately increasing our chances of achieving success.

Success is not a solitary pursuit; it is a journey that often requires unwavering commitment and perseverance. In times of doubt or hardship, having a supportive partner by our side can make all the difference. Partners provide encouragement, lend an empathetic ear, and offer valuable advice when we face obstacles. They help us navigate through challenging moments and offer a shoulder to lean on. Through the power of partnership, we gain the emotional strength and resilience needed to weather the storms and stay focused on our goals.

Partnerships extend beyond the immediate bond between individuals. They create networks of interconnected relationships, amplifying our reach and influence. Through partnerships, we gain access to a broader audience, resources, and opportunities that would otherwise be beyond our grasp. By leveraging these networks, we can accelerate progress, unlock new doors, and achieve success more rapidly. The connections forged through partnerships pave the way for collaboration with other like-minded individuals, expanding our horizons even further.

Partnerships foster a sense of mutual accountability, challenging us to perform at our best and remain committed to our shared objectives. When we have someone relying on us, we become more driven, disciplined, and focused. Partnerships hold us accountable for our actions and choices, compelling us to rise above mediocrity and strive for excellence. The presence of a partner encourages us to set higher standards and push our boundaries, leading to personal and collective growth.

In a world that often celebrates individual accomplishments, we must recognize the profound impact of partnerships on our journey towards success. From business ventures to personal aspirations, the power of partnership permeates every facet of our lives. By joining forces, we unlock the potential for collaboration, shared knowledge, emotional support, and expanded networks. Together, we can achieve greatness that surpasses what any one person can accomplish alone. As we embrace the power of partnership, we embrace the boundless opportunities it offers, propelling us to new heights and realizing our fullest potential.

Partnerships have a remarkable ability to generate synergy and foster innovation. When diverse minds collaborate, they bring together a range of perspectives, ideas, and approaches.

This diversity sparks creativity and promotes out-of-the-box thinking, leading to breakthrough innovations and solutions. Partnerships encourage the exploration of new possibilities, challenging traditional ways of doing things and inspiring fresh perspectives. Through the power of collaboration, we can combine our strengths and insights to create something truly extraordinary.

Partnerships allow us to leverage collective resources and achieve more significant outcomes. Whether it's financial resources, technological advancements, or physical assets, pooling resources with a partner amplifies our capacity to make an impact. Together, we can access funding, equipment, networks, and expertise that may not be readily available to us individually. By joining forces, we maximize our potential and unlock opportunities that might have otherwise been out of reach.

In a rapidly evolving world, adaptability and resilience are critical factors for success. Partnerships provide a support system that helps us navigate through uncertainty and change. When faced with unexpected challenges or shifting circumstances, partners can offer valuable insights, alternative perspectives, and innovative strategies. They provide a stabilizing force and can help us pivot, adjust, and thrive in the face of adversity. Through partnerships, we gain the flexibility and resilience needed to navigate the complexities of the ever-changing world.

Partnerships create a shared sense of accomplishment and celebration. When we achieve success together, the joy and satisfaction are magnified. By sharing the journey and reaching milestones collectively, partnerships create a sense of camaraderie, unity, and fulfillment. The success becomes more meaningful as it is not just an individual triumph but a shared victory. Partnerships foster a culture of support, collaboration, and mutual celebration, strengthening the bonds between individuals and propelling them towards even greater achievements.

Partnerships have the power to leave a lasting legacy that extends far beyond our individual contributions. By working together towards a shared vision, we can create enduring impact and inspire future generations. Partnerships enable us to tackle grand challenges, address societal issues, and make a significant difference in the world. When we combine our efforts, we can create a ripple effect that extends far beyond our immediate sphere of influence, leaving a positive and lasting legacy for years to come.

The power of partnership is undeniable. It empowers us to leverage our strengths, share knowledge, provide emotional support, expand networks, and achieve success beyond our individual capacities. Through partnerships, we create synergy, foster innovation, and unlock new possibilities. The impact of partnerships extends beyond our immediate goals, leaving a lasting legacy and inspiring others to collaborate and pursue their dreams. As we recognize and harness the power of partnership, we open ourselves up to a world of boundless potential and endless opportunities for growth, achievement, and collective success.

Partnerships provide a crucial support system during times of failure or setbacks. In the pursuit of success, it is inevitable to face challenges and experience failures along the way. However, having a partner by your side can help you navigate through these difficult times. Partners offer encouragement, perspective, and valuable lessons learned from their own experiences. They remind you that failure is not the end but an opportunity to learn, grow, and recalibrate your approach. Through partnerships, we gain resilience, learn from mistakes, and become better equipped to overcome obstacles on the path to success.

Partnerships introduce us to diverse perspectives and broaden our worldview. When we collaborate with others, especially those from different backgrounds, cultures, or areas of expertise, we gain fresh insights and alternative viewpoints. These different perspectives challenge our assumptions, ignite creativity, and encourage us to consider new possibilities. By embracing diversity within partnerships, we cultivate a rich and inclusive environment that fosters innovation and leads to more comprehensive and impactful solutions.

Successful partnerships rely on a balance of roles and responsibilities. Each partner brings their unique strengths, abilities, and perspectives to the table, allowing for a well-rounded approach to achieving shared goals. By distributing tasks and responsibilities based on individual strengths, partnerships maximize efficiency and productivity. This balance creates a harmonious synergy where partners can focus on what they do best while trusting and relying on their counterparts to excel in their respective areas. Through effective role balancing, partnerships become a powerful force for success.

Partnerships are built on trust, respect, and open communication. Trust forms the foundation of successful collaborations, allowing partners to rely on each other's expertise, judgment, and support. Trust fosters a safe environment where ideas can be freely shared, feedback can be given and received constructively, and conflicts can be resolved effectively. Collaboration thrives when partners feel valued, respected, and empowered. By nurturing trust within partnerships, we create a fertile ground for innovation, growth, and shared success.

Partnerships have a ripple effect that extends beyond the immediate individuals involved. When we experience the power and benefits of successful partnerships, we are inspired to pay it forward and help others succeed. By sharing our knowledge, resources, and experiences, we can become catalysts for collaboration and contribute to the success of others. The spirit of partnership spreads, creating a supportive ecosystem where individuals lift each other up, share opportunities, and collaborate for mutual growth and achievement.

Partnerships are a cornerstone of success, enabling us to achieve greater heights than we could ever reach alone. They bring together complementary strengths, foster innovation, provide emotional support, and expand networks. Partnerships teach us resilience, challenge our perspectives, and create a culture of collaboration and shared celebration. As we recognize and embrace the power of partnership, we unlock endless possibilities for growth, achievement, and making a positive impact on the world. Together, we can accomplish extraordinary feats and leave a lasting legacy that inspires others to forge their own partnerships and unlock their full potential.

In today's digital age, the internet has revolutionized the way we connect, communicate, and collaborate. The power of online collaboration has opened up vast opportunities for individuals to build success, create impact, and achieve their goals. In this chapter, we will explore how to harness the power of online collaboration to build success and thrive in the digital realm.

To utilize online collaboration effectively, start by clarifying your vision and setting clear goals.

Determine what you want to achieve and identify the areas where collaboration can enhance your efforts. Whether it's launching a business, developing a project, or creating content, a well-defined vision serves as a roadmap for collaboration and aligns partners towards a common purpose.

Online collaboration thrives on the right platforms and tools that facilitate communication, sharing, and teamwork. Research and identify platforms and tools that suit your specific needs, such as project management tools, communication platforms, file sharing services, and online networking communities. Consider factors like user-friendliness, security, and scalability to ensure a seamless collaboration experience.

Building success online requires connecting with like-minded individuals who share your goals and interests. Join relevant online communities, forums, and social media groups where you can meet potential collaborators. Engage in discussions, share your expertise, and actively seek out individuals who align with your vision. Cultivate relationships with individuals who complement your skills and bring diverse perspectives to the table.

Establishing trust and effective communication is vital in online collaborations. Foster an environment of open communication, where ideas and feedback are welcomed. Establish clear channels of communication, whether it's through video conferencing, chat platforms, or email. Be responsive, reliable, and transparent in your interactions to build trust with your collaborators. Regularly update your partners on progress, seek their input, and encourage open dialogue to strengthen the collaboration.

Clearly defining roles and responsibilities ensures that each collaborator knows their specific contributions and expectations. Assign tasks based on individual strengths and expertise, allowing everyone to focus on what they do best. Establish a system for tracking progress, deadlines, and deliverables to maintain accountability. By clarifying roles, you streamline workflows, maximize productivity, and create a harmonious collaboration experience.

Online collaborations thrive on diverse perspectives and collaboration. Embrace different backgrounds, experiences, and expertise within your collaborative team. Encourage creativity, innovation, and out-of-the-box thinking by fostering an inclusive environment. Create opportunities for brainstorming sessions, idea-sharing, and collaborative problem-solving. By valuing and respecting diverse contributions, you can unlock unique solutions and fuel success.

Online collaborations provide a wealth of opportunities for continuous learning and growth. Encourage knowledge sharing among collaborators through webinars, workshops, and resource sharing. Embrace a mindset of curiosity, staying updated with industry trends, and exploring new technologies and techniques. Foster a culture of feedback and learning from both successes and failures. Embracing continuous learning empowers collaborators to stay ahead, innovate, and adapt to the ever-changing digital landscape.

Leverage the power of online collaboration to expand your network and reach a wider audience. Collaborate with influencers, experts, or individuals with larger followings to amplify your message and build brand awareness. Guest posting, cross-promotion, and collaborative content creation are effective ways to tap into new audiences and leverage each other's networks. By leveraging the collective reach of your collaborators, you can increase your visibility and attract new opportunities.

Online collaborations offer flexibility and agility, allowing you to adapt quickly to changing circumstances. Embrace the benefits of remote work, flexible schedules, and global collaboration. Leverage online project management tools to track progress, manage tasks, and adjust timelines as needed. Be open to new ideas and be willing to pivot if necessary. By embracing flexibility and agility, you can navigate challenges, seize opportunities, and maintain momentum towards success.

Celebrating milestones and recognizing the contributions of your collaborators is essential for maintaining motivation and fostering a positive collaboration experience. Acknowledge and appreciate the efforts and achievements of your team members regularly. Provide constructive feedback, highlight successes, and publicly recognize individual and collective accomplishments. Celebrating together strengthens the bond among collaborators and encourages a sense of pride and shared ownership.

Online collaborations have the potential to extend beyond individual projects. Focus on building long-term relationships with your collaborators. Cultivate genuine connections, provide ongoing support, and explore opportunities for future collaborations. By nurturing relationships, you create a network of trusted partners who can support each other's growth, refer new opportunities, and continue to collaborate on future endeavors.

After each collaborative project, take time to reflect on the experience and extract valuable lessons. Assess what worked well, what challenges arose, and how the collaboration could be improved in the future. Encourage open and honest feedback from all participants to foster continuous improvement. Apply the insights gained to refine your collaborative approach and enhance future endeavors.

The power of online collaboration is a game-changer in today's digital landscape. By harnessing the potential of technology, connecting with like-minded individuals, and embracing diversity, you can build success online. Foster trust, effective communication, and collaboration, and leverage the resources and opportunities that arise from online platforms. Embrace flexibility, continuous learning, and celebrate achievements together. Through online collaboration, you can expand your reach, innovate, and achieve success that surpasses what you could accomplish alone. Embrace the power of online collaboration, and unlock your full potential in the digital realm.

Online collaboration allows for iterative processes and continuous improvement. Embrace a culture of iteration, where ideas are refined through feedback and constructive criticism. Encourage active participation and create a safe space for collaborators to share their thoughts openly. Actively seek feedback from your team and be open to incorporating their suggestions. Iteration based on feedback helps refine strategies, optimize workflows, and drive towards greater success.

The digital realm offers a wealth of data and analytics that can enhance online collaborations. Utilize analytics tools to gain insights into user behavior, market trends, and performance metrics. Leverage this data to make informed decisions, refine your strategies, and identify areas for improvement. By leveraging data, you can optimize your online collaboration efforts and achieve greater success.

As you achieve success through online collaboration, remember to give back to the online community that supports you. Share your knowledge and experiences through blog posts, webinars, or online tutorials. Actively engage with others in online communities by answering questions, providing guidance, and offering support. By contributing positively to the online community, you establish yourself as a trusted collaborator and foster goodwill that can lead to future opportunities.

The digital landscape is ever-evolving, so it's crucial to stay agile and embrace innovation. Keep up with emerging technologies, trends, and tools that can enhance your online collaboration efforts. Be open to trying new approaches, experimenting with different strategies, and adapting to changes in the online environment. By staying agile and embracing innovation, you can stay ahead of the curve and maintain a competitive edge.

Online collaborations thrive in a positive and inclusive culture. Foster an environment where everyone feels valued, respected, and heard. Embrace diversity and create space for different perspectives, experiences, and backgrounds. Encourage collaboration, teamwork, and mutual support among your online collaborators. By fostering a positive and inclusive culture, you create a collaborative environment where everyone can thrive and contribute to collective success.

Online collaborations provide the opportunity for individuals to work autonomously while still collaborating effectively. Balance the need for individual autonomy with the benefits of collaboration. Provide collaborators with the freedom to work independently, allowing them to bring their unique skills and expertise to the table. At the same time, create opportunities for collaboration, knowledge sharing, and collective decision-making. Balancing autonomy and collaboration ensures a harmonious and productive online collaboration experience.

The digital landscape is dynamic, and online collaboration strategies must adapt and evolve accordingly. Continuously evaluate the effectiveness of your online collaboration efforts and be willing to make necessary adjustments. Stay informed about emerging technologies, trends, and best practices in online collaboration. Embrace a growth mindset and be open to learning from both successes and failures. By continuously adapting and evolving, you can leverage the full potential of online collaboration to drive long-term success.

Harnessing the power of online collaboration is instrumental in building success in the digital realm. By leveraging technology, embracing diversity, nurturing relationships, and fostering a positive and inclusive culture, you can create impactful collaborations that drive towards your goals. Stay agile, innovate, and adapt to the ever-changing online landscape. Embrace data and feedback, give back to the online community, and balance autonomy with collaboration. With a strategic approach and a commitment to continuous improvement, you can unlock the full potential of online collaboration and achieve remarkable success in the digital world.

Your Online Empire

As the digital landscape continues to evolve, opportunities for building online empires have become more accessible than ever before. The internet has given rise to countless success stories, with individuals creating thriving businesses and achieving financial independence. If you have a burning desire to build your own online empire, this chapter is dedicated to showing you that it's not only possible but also within your reach. By following your instincts and taking a step of faith, you can embark on an extraordinary journey of building a successful online venture.

Deep within you lies an inherent power - your instincts. Your instincts are the compass that guides you toward your true purpose. Trusting your instincts is the first step towards building an online empire. Take a moment to reflect on what truly inspires and motivates you. What subjects or industries spark a fire within you? By listening to your instincts, you can identify the areas where your passion and expertise align.

The internet has revolutionized the way we live, work, and connect with others. It has created a vast playground of opportunities for those who dare to explore it. Embrace the digital landscape and immerse yourself in its possibilities. Research emerging trends, study successful online businesses, and familiarize yourself with the tools and technologies available. The more you understand the online world, the better equipped you'll be to navigate and seize the opportunities that come your way.

In a crowded online marketplace, it's crucial to differentiate yourself from the competition.

Identify your unique value proposition - the qualities, skills, or products that set you apart. What can you offer that others can't? Is it your expertise, innovative ideas, exceptional customer service, or a combination of factors? Find your niche and position yourself as an expert or leader in that area.

Building an online empire requires a willingness to take risks and step outside your comfort zone. Taking a leap of faith may feel daunting, but remember that great rewards often come from calculated risks. Embrace the uncertainty and trust in your abilities. Start small if needed, and gradually expand as you gain confidence and experience. Trust that the universe has a way of aligning circumstances in your favor when you pursue your passions with authenticity and dedication.

The online world moves at a rapid pace, and to build a successful empire, you must be willing to continuously learn and adapt. Stay informed about industry trends, consumer behavior, and technological advancements. Be open to experimenting with new strategies and approaches. Embrace failure as a learning opportunity and refine your tactics based on the lessons learned. Remember, an online empire is built on the foundation of adaptability and growth.

Surround yourself with like-minded individuals who share your vision and ambition. Seek out collaboration opportunities and build relationships within your industry. Connect with mentors or experts who have already achieved success in the online realm. Their guidance and insights can prove invaluable as you navigate the challenges and triumphs of building your empire. Remember, no empire is built alone; it takes a network of supporters to truly thrive.

Building an online empire is not an overnight journey; it requires perseverance. There will be obstacles, setbacks, and moments of doubt. But it's crucial to keep pushing forward, even when the path seems uncertain. Believe in yourself and the vision you have for your online empire. Trust that each step, even the smallest ones, contributes to the greater picture you have in mind. Embrace challenges as opportunities for growth and view setbacks as valuable lessons that shape your path towards success.

While following your instincts and taking a step of faith are essential, it's equally important to create a solid plan. A well-thought-out strategy will provide you with a roadmap for success. Define your goals, break them down into actionable steps, and establish timelines for achieving them. Be diligent in executing your plan, but also remain flexible and adaptable as circumstances change along the way.

In the digital era, effective marketing is key to building an online empire. Leverage the power of digital marketing tools and techniques to reach your target audience and make a lasting impact. Invest time in understanding your customers' needs, desires, and online behavior. Develop a strong online presence through engaging content, search engine optimization, social media marketing, and other relevant channels. Build a community around your brand and foster meaningful connections with your audience.

As your online empire begins to flourish, consider scaling and diversifying your business. Explore new avenues, products, or services that align with your core values and target audience. Expand your reach by collaborating with influencers, exploring strategic partnerships, or even venturing into new markets. Remember, a dynamic and evolving empire is more likely to withstand the ever-changing digital landscape.

As you achieve success and build your online empire, remember the importance of giving back and paying it forward. Share your knowledge, expertise, and resources with others who are aspiring to create their own online ventures. Support causes and initiatives that align with your values. By making a positive impact, you not only leave a lasting legacy but also attract abundance and fulfillment into your own life.

Building an online empire is an exhilarating adventure, filled with highs, lows, and unexpected twists. Embrace the journey with an open mind and heart. Celebrate your victories, learn from your failures, and savor every milestone along the way. Trust that the universe is guiding you towards your ultimate destiny, and have faith in your ability to create something extraordinary.

Remember, building an online empire is a testament to your courage, determination, and belief in your own potential. Trust your instincts, take a step of faith, and embark on this transformative journey. The online world is waiting for you to leave your mark and create a legacy that will inspire others for generations to come.

In the pursuit of building an online empire, it's crucial to cultivate a mindset of abundance. Believe in your ability to achieve success and attract opportunities. Banish limiting beliefs and replace them with empowering thoughts. Embrace a positive outlook, resilience, and a sense of gratitude for the progress you make along the way. Remember, abundance begets abundance, and by embodying a mindset of success, you invite greater prosperity into your life and your empire.

As you devote yourself to building an online empire, it's essential to prioritize self-care. Entrepreneurship can be demanding, both mentally and physically. Take care of your well-being by maintaining a healthy work-life balance. Nurture your mind, body, and spirit through regular exercise, proper nutrition, and mindfulness practices. Find activities that rejuvenate and inspire you, allowing you to recharge and sustain your entrepreneurial spirit for the long haul.

The online landscape is ever-evolving, with new technologies and trends emerging at a rapid pace. To stay ahead and maintain your empire's relevance, embrace innovation and adaptability. Keep a finger on the pulse of industry advancements and consumer preferences. Explore emerging technologies, such as artificial intelligence, virtual reality, or blockchain, and assess how they can enhance your business model. By embracing change and being open to new ideas, you position your empire at the forefront of innovation.

Along your journey of building an online empire, take the time to celebrate milestones and reflect on how far you've come. Acknowledge your accomplishments, no matter how small they may seem. Celebrate the wins, the breakthroughs, and the lessons learned. Allow yourself to bask in the joy and fulfillment that comes from building something meaningful. Taking the time to appreciate your progress will fuel your motivation and inspire you to reach even greater heights.

Amidst the vast digital landscape, it's easy to lose sight of your true self. However, authenticity should be the foundation of your online empire. Stay true to your values, purpose, and unique voice. Let your passion and genuine connection with your audience shine through in every interaction. By staying authentic, you build trust and loyalty, fostering a community that will stand by your side as your empire grows.

Building an online empire is a lifelong journey of learning and growth. Commit yourself to continuous education and personal development. Stay curious and hungry for knowledge in your field. Seek out mentors, attend conferences, read books, and engage in communities where you can learn from others. Embrace the mindset of a perpetual student, and your online empire will remain at the forefront of innovation and success.

As your online empire thrives, remember the power you hold to empower others. Use your influence and resources to make a positive impact in the lives of those around you. Give back to your community, support causes that align with your values, and create opportunities for others to succeed. By lifting others up, you create a ripple effect of positivity and contribute to a world where online empires are built not just for personal gain, but to uplift humanity as a whole.

Ultimately, building an online empire is not solely about the destination; it's about the journey itself. Embrace the process, the challenges, the growth, and the triumphs. Find joy and fulfillment in every step, knowing that you are creating something remarkable and leaving a legacy for generations to come.

to come. Embrace the joy of creating, innovating, and connecting with your audience. Celebrate the relationships you form, the impact you make, and the sense of purpose that comes from building your online empire.

As you build your online empire, remember that success is not defined solely by financial gains or the size of your following. It is a holistic measure that encompasses fulfillment, authenticity, and the positive impact you have on others. Stay connected to your passion, your instincts, and the core values that drive you. With each step you take and each decision you make, let your intuition be your guide, for it is often the whispers of your soul leading you towards your true calling.

Believe in yourself, trust the journey, and know that building an online empire is within your reach. It may require dedication, resilience, and a leap of faith, but the possibilities are boundless. The digital world offers endless opportunities for growth, impact, and fulfillment. So, go forth, follow your instincts, take that step of faith, and watch as you build an extraordinary online empire that leaves a lasting legacy. Your empire awaits—now it's time to make your mark on the digital realm.

Engaging Your Audience

The audience matters. In the realm of entertainment, successful showmen possess a unique ability to captivate and engage their audiences. Whether they are performers, presenters, or public speakers, these individuals have mastered the art of drawing people into their world and leaving a lasting impact. In this chapter, we will explore the techniques and characteristics that make showmen successful at engaging their audiences.

One crucial aspect of captivating an audience is understanding who they are. Successful showmen invest time and effort in researching their target audience to identify their preferences, interests, and expectations. By gaining insights into their audience's desires, showmen can tailor their performances to meet those expectations, creating a deeper connection from the outset.

A fundamental skill possessed by successful showmen is the ability to tell compelling stories. They understand that storytelling is a powerful tool to engage emotions and create a lasting impact on the audience. Showmen weave narratives that resonate with their audience's experiences, using vivid imagery, relatable characters, and captivating plotlines. Through effective storytelling, they transport their audience into an immersive world where they become emotionally invested.

Authenticity is key to establishing trust and rapport with an audience. Successful showmen embrace their unique personalities, allowing their true selves to shine through their performances. They connect with their audience by sharing personal anecdotes, vulnerabilities, and experiences, fostering an atmosphere of genuine connection. By being authentic, showmen create a relatable and trustworthy persona that resonates with the audience.

Showmen possess a magnetic stage presence that draws the audience's attention from the moment they step on stage. They exude confidence, enthusiasm, and energy, which radiate throughout the crowd, creating a contagious atmosphere. Their body language, gestures, and facial expressions are carefully crafted to engage and captivate the audience. By utilizing their charisma, showmen effortlessly command the stage and hold their audience's attention.

Successful showmen understand the importance of interaction in engaging audiences. They actively involve the audience through various techniques such as audience participation, Q&A sessions, or interactive demonstrations. By allowing the audience to become an active part of the performance, showmen create a sense of inclusion and excitement. These interactive elements keep the audience engaged, as they feel personally invested in the experience.

In today's digital age, successful showmen harness the power of technology to enhance their performances. They incorporate multimedia elements, such as audiovisual effects, lighting, and stage props, to create visually stunning and immersive experiences. Showmen also leverage social media platforms and live streaming to expand their reach and connect with audiences beyond the physical confines of a venue. By embracing technology, showmen amplify their ability to engage and leave a lasting impression on their audience.

The art of captivating and engaging an audience is a multifaceted skill that successful showmen possess. By understanding their audience, mastering the art of storytelling, being authentic, exuding charisma, incorporating interactive elements, and utilizing technology, these showmen create unforgettable experiences. Their ability to draw in and engage audiences is a testament to their dedication, creativity, and passion for their craft. Aspiring showmen can learn from these techniques and develop their own unique style to captivate audiences and make a lasting impact in the world of entertainment.

In the digital age, establishing a strong online presence is crucial for success in various domains, including business, entrepreneurship, content creation, and personal branding. However, merely existing online is not enough. To truly thrive in the virtual realm, individuals and organizations must actively engage with their online audience. In this chapter, we will explore the importance of engaging with your online audience to achieve success on the internet.

Engagement fosters the development of meaningful relationships with your online audience. By actively interacting with your followers, responding to their comments, and acknowledging their contributions, you establish a sense of connection and trust. Building these relationships creates a loyal and dedicated community that not only supports you but also advocates for your brand or content.

Engagement provides invaluable insights into the needs, preferences, and opinions of your online audience. By actively listening to their feedback, participating in discussions, and conducting surveys or polls, you gain a deeper understanding of what your audience wants. This knowledge allows you to tailor your content, products, or services to better meet their expectations, thereby increasing your chances of success.

The internet can often feel impersonal, but engagement allows you to bridge that gap and create a personal connection with your online audience. Showcasing your authenticity, sharing personal stories, and being responsive to their comments and messages humanizes your online presence. This personal connection strengthens the bond between you and your audience, making them feel more invested in your journey and more likely to support you.

Engaging with your online audience encourages them to become active participants in your online ecosystem. By soliciting user-generated content, such as reviews, testimonials, or creative contributions, you empower your audience to be part of the content creation process. This not only builds a sense of community but also amplifies your reach as your audience shares their contributions with their own networks, expanding your online visibility and potential for success.

Engagement plays a pivotal role in transforming your audience into loyal brand advocates. When you consistently engage with your audience, respond to their queries, and provide value through your content or offerings, they are more likely to become ambassadors for your brand. Satisfied and engaged followers are more inclined to recommend your brand, share your content, and defend your reputation, ultimately contributing to your online success.

Engagement helps you stay attuned to the ever-evolving digital landscape. By actively participating in online conversations, monitoring trends, and seeking feedback, you can adapt your strategies and offerings to align with the changing preferences and demands of your audience. This agility and responsiveness enable you to remain relevant in the online sphere and maintain a competitive edge.

In the vast and ever-expanding realm of the internet, engagement with your online audience is crucial for achieving success. Building relationships, understanding audience needs, creating personal connections, driving user-generated content, increasing brand advocacy, and staying relevant are all outcomes of active engagement. By dedicating time and effort to nurture your online community, you lay the foundation for sustainable growth, increased visibility, and the realization of your goals in the digital landscape. Embrace the power of engagement, and unlock the true potential of your online endeavors.

Social media platforms have revolutionized the way we engage with our online audience. These platforms provide a fertile ground for interaction, allowing you to connect with your audience on a personal level. Utilize the features offered by social media platforms, such as comments, direct messages, live videos, and polls, to actively engage with your followers. Regularly respond to comments and messages, initiate conversations, and share valuable content that sparks discussion. By leveraging the power of social media, you can build a vibrant online community and propel your success.

Engaging with your online audience goes beyond mere interactions. It involves consistently providing value and showcasing your expertise. Share insightful and informative content that addresses your audience's pain points, answers their questions, and offers practical solutions. By positioning yourself as a trusted source of knowledge and expertise, you become a go-to resource for your audience. This not only enhances your credibility but also keeps your audience engaged and hungry for more.

Successful online engagement is a two-way street. While it's essential to actively communicate with your audience, it's equally important to listen and acknowledge their perspectives. Encourage dialogue, ask for feedback, and actively consider their suggestions. Actively participating in discussions and incorporating feedback shows that you value your audience's opinions, fostering a sense of inclusivity and fostering a strong sense of community.

Consistency is key when it comes to engaging with your online audience. Establish a regular posting schedule and maintain a consistent presence across your chosen online platforms. Consistency builds trust and reliability, keeping your audience engaged and expecting more from you. Furthermore, authenticity is paramount in your interactions. Be genuine, transparent, and true to yourself. Authenticity resonates with your audience and creates a connection that is difficult to replicate.

To fine-tune your engagement strategies, it's essential to analyze the metrics and insights provided by the various online platforms. Pay attention to metrics such as reach, engagement rate, click-through rate, and audience demographics. These metrics offer valuable insights into what content resonates with your audience, the optimal times to engage, and the platforms that yield the best results. Use this information to refine your approach and amplify your success.

As your online presence grows and evolves, so does your audience. Stay attuned to their changing needs, interests, and preferences. Continuously adapt your strategies and content to align with their evolving expectations. Engage in market research, conduct surveys, and seek direct feedback to understand your audience better. By proactively evolving with your audience, you maintain relevance and ensure continued success in the online realm.

Engaging with your online audience is not just a strategy; it's a mindset. It requires an ongoing commitment to building relationships, providing value, and nurturing a thriving online community. By harnessing the power of social media, showcasing authenticity, embracing two-way communication, maintaining consistency, analyzing metrics, and adapting to your audience's needs, you pave the way for sustained success on the internet. Remember, engagement is not just about numbers; it's about forging meaningful connections, making a positive impact, and fostering a dedicated following that will support you on your journey to online success.

The Future of the Internet

The Internet, a global network of interconnected computers, has witnessed a remarkable evolution since its inception. From its humble beginnings as a research project to its ubiquitous presence in every aspect of modern life, the Internet has undergone significant transformations over the years. In this chapter, we will delve into the key milestones that have shaped the Internet as we know it today.

The story of the Internet starts in the 1960s with the Advanced Research Projects Agency Network (ARPANET), a network developed by the U.S. Department of Defense. Initially designed for military purposes, ARPANET connected various research institutions and universities. It introduced packet-switching technology, which allowed data to be broken down into smaller packets and transmitted across different routes, ensuring robustness and reliability.

While the early Internet focused on connecting computers, it was the invention of the World Wide Web in 1989 by Sir Tim Berners-Lee that revolutionized communication and information sharing. The Web introduced the concept of hyperlinks, allowing users to navigate between interconnected web pages. The advent of web browsers, such as Mosaic and later Netscape Navigator, made the Internet more accessible and user-friendly.

The 1990s witnessed a surge of commercial activity on the Internet, commonly known as the dot-com boom. Many companies began to realize the Internet's potential for e-commerce and established online stores and services. This period saw the rise and fall of numerous startups, with investors pouring vast amounts of money into Internet-based ventures. While the dot-com bubble eventually burst in the early 2000s, it laid the foundation for the online business landscape we see today.

In the late 1990s and early 2000s, dial-up connections dominated the Internet landscape. However, the introduction of broadband technologies, such as Digital Subscriber Line (DSL) and cable internet, revolutionized Internet access. Broadband provided significantly faster and always-on connections, enabling users to consume media-rich content, stream videos, and participate in online gaming. This advancement paved the way for the widespread adoption of the Internet in households worldwide.

The next major milestone in Internet evolution came with the proliferation of mobile devices and the advent of smartphones. With the introduction of the iPhone in 2007 and subsequent Android-based devices, people gained access to the Internet through their pockets. Mobile data networks, such as 3G and later 4G, allowed for fast and reliable Internet access on the go. This led to a mobile revolution, transforming the way we communicate, consume information, and interact with the digital world.

The rise of social media platforms, such as Facebook, Twitter, and Instagram, brought about a paradigm shift in Internet usage. These platforms allowed users to create, share, and engage with content on a massive scale. The democratization of information empowered individuals and sparked social movements worldwide. Social media also became a prominent avenue for businesses to connect with their audiences and advertise their products and services.

ABOUT THE AUTHOR

Dr. Jeremy Lopez is Founder and President of Identity Network and Now Is Your Moment. Identity Network is one of the world's leading prophetic resource sites, offering books, teachings, and courses to a global audience. For more than thirty years, Dr. Lopez has been considered a pioneering voice within the field of the prophetic arts and his proven strategies for success coaching are now being implemented by various training groups and faith groups throughout the world. Dr. Lopez is the author of more than forty books, including his international bestselling books The Universe is at Your Command and Creating with Your Thoughts. Throughout his career, he has spoken prophetically into the lives of heads of business as well as heads of state. He has ministered to Governor Bob Riley of the State of Alabama, Prime Minister Benjamin Netanyahu, and Shimon Peres. Dr. Lopez continues to be a highly sought conference teacher and host, speaking on the topics of human potential and spirituality.